# THE CONSTITUTION
# AND WORLD ORGANIZATION

# THE CONSTITUTION
## AND
# WORLD ORGANIZATION

BY EDWARD S. CORWIN

**BOOKS FOR LIBRARIES PRESS**
FREEPORT, NEW YORK

STANDARD BOOK NUMBER:
8369-5322-3


LIBRARY OF CONGRESS CATALOG CARD NUMBER:
73-117869


PRINTED IN THE UNITED STATES OF AMERICA

# FOREWORD

THE American people are overwhelmingly of the opinion at the present time that the controlling objective of our foreign policy following upon the close of the war ought to be to "seek peace and ensue it." A considerable majority go further and hold that such a policy can be prosecuted most successfully, and most beneficially for the rest of the world as well as ourselves, through membership in an international organization for the promotion of peace among the nations, great and small. But what form ought such an organization take? When this question is approached a wide diversity of opinion becomes manifest. Nor does this study aim to deal with that question. I have been content merely to show that the Constitution leaves it with American public opinion to determine on the basis of today's need what commitments our Government shall make in behalf of international peace.

I wish to take this opportunity to thank Professor Arthur O. Lovejoy of the Universities Committee on Post-War International Problems, and my colleague Professor John B. Whitton for several suggestions which proved of value in the final revision of this study. For its remaining deficiencies I alone am to blame.

EDWARD S. CORWIN

Princeton
February 22, 1944

# CONTENTS

# INTRODUCTION

It is the major purpose of this study to inquire whether the Constitution, as it is today interpreted and applied in the field of foreign relations, puts any special or peculiar difficulties in the way of entrance by the United States into an international organization for the maintenance of peace; or, in other words, whether there is anything about our Constitutional Law and the structure of our government that denies us, either theoretically or in fact, a free hand to promote world peace in the years to come. A secondary inquiry is whether the concept of national sovereignty does this.

The principal question naturally suggests a comparison with the institutions of other countries, but any such comparison, I feel persuaded, would be of little worth. To take the U.S.S.R., where the primary purpose of institutions, both political and otherwise, is the effectuation of a dictator's will, as furnishing a relevant standard would be obviously absurd, and the more so since no one is proposing that we would, should, or could abandon our democratic procedures in order to facilitate our entrance into an international organization. If, on the other hand, we should take the British Cabinet system as furnishing the best example of an efficiently functioning democracy, we should invite disappointment of a different sort. For while the British Cabinet system and our own Presidential system naturally give rise to divergent methods in the conduct of foreign relations, these differences are apt to be too much entangled with imponderables of tradition and accidents of personality to be separately assessable for their effects. Nor, again, does anybody seem to be seriously suggesting that we ought presently to exchange our system for the British system as part of the price of admission into a new international order.

Yet that there are certain distinctive features of the American constitutional system whose presence is calculated to render the conduct of foreign relations by our government a more difficult matter than it would otherwise be, no one would deny, and especially these two features: (1) What are termed Constitutional Limitations on the powers of the National Government; (2) the rule governing the participation of the Senate in treaty-making. The potentialities of the former have been demonstrated negatively for the most part, by the watering down which Constitutional Limitations on national power have, first and last, undergone at the hands of the Supreme Court when it has been invited to give them their logical application in the field of foreign relations; and the potentialities of the Senate's treaty-making role have been demonstrated again and again. Today, nevertheless, the Senate's role is definitely challenged, and partly in consequence of the watering down, just mentioned, of Constitutional Limitations in the diplomatic field. The connection, therefore, between the present status of Constitutional Limitations in that field and the present health of the Senate's treaty-making agency is close. It is also important, as the reader will learn in due course.

More specifically, I shall endeavor in the following pages to answer with such degree of precision and definiteness as I can summon to my aid the following questions:

I. Does the concept of National Sovereignty set limits logically to entrance by the United States into an international organization?

II. Does the Constitution of the United States offer difficulties thereto in consequence:

    A. of the concept of Dual Federalism;

    B. of the principle of the Separation of Powers;

    C. of the limitations which it imposes on the powers of the National Government in favor of private rights;

    D. of adding to the international engagements of the United States a *constitutional* sanction, so that the type of international agreement here in contemplation would seriously reduce the *constitutional* freedom of action of the National Government in comparison with that of other governments?

III. How serious a constitutional obstacle does the role of the Senate in treaty-making today interpose to entrance by the United States into an international organization?

We shall consider these topics in order.

# I. SOVEREIGNTY

PROBABLY no term known to political science has been more variously defined than "sovereignty," but whatever definition of it is adopted, it must be evident that the United States can hardly claim to be *more* "sovereign" than several other nations which a viable international organization must include, Great Britain and Russia, for example. Clearly, to take the position that the United States could not because of its *sovereignty* accept obligations which Great Britain and Russia were able to accept, would lead to the paradox that the United States was actually less sovereign than they, less capable of forming international relationships. Question I, nevertheless, may not be dismissed in quite this cavalier fashion, embodying as it does issues which have long troubled both theorists and practical men and which on that score at least demand some passing notice.

Three possible conceptions of sovereignty which have bearing on the problem here under discussion are suggested by the pertinent literature of the subject: (1) National Sovereignty may be regarded as a concept of International Law and hence as limited by the obligations which that law imposes upon members of the Family of Nations, including the obligation to observe their contractual engagements with one another.

Or (2), it may be held that "sovereignty" is an inherent characteristic of state existence as such, which is anterior to International Law and membership in the Family of Nations, and which leaves its possessors always free in the last analysis to determine on the basis of interest alone the extent to which they shall observe the requirements of International Law and of their engagements to other nations. Or, in more concrete terms, a *sovereign* nation is bound by International Law and by the international conventions to which it is party only to the extent that those who determine its foreign relations think expedient at any moment.

Or (3), it may be held that "national sovereignty" so-called is merely an honorific term for such powers as the Family of Nations has seen fit from time to time to bestow upon its several members; that, in other words, the Family of Nations is the only *real* sovereign, and that the so-called sovereign nations are in the contemplation of International Law merely its organs and appendages.

This is the view, for example, of "the Austrian School" of which Professors Kelsen and Verdross have been in recent times the outstanding spokesmen.[1] Inasmuch as this view logically interposes no difficulties in the way of even a complete mergence of existing national "sovereignties" into a World State, it may for our purposes be dismissed with a brief word. When set over against the actual record of the relations of the Great Powers during the last three hundred years, this theory is seen to be a *tour de force* of heroic rationalization directed toward a selected ideal, and little else. By the same token, it provides a ready-made rationalization for any pretensions to power which an actual organization of the states of the world may be able someday to assert in actual practice. The importance of this theory therefore, if it has any, lies in future possible developments in the international field. For our purposes it is negligible.

Theory (1), above, possesses, on the other hand, very impressive historical support. This theory asserts that International Law itself imposes certain limits on the sovereignty, and hence on the freedom of action of members of the Family of Nations, and that every nation upon its entrance into the Family of Nations consents to be bound by those limits and continues thus bound so long as it remains a member of the Family of Nations. Such limits are accordingly essential ingredients of each nation's sovereignty—sovereignty, in short, exists *within* International Law and the international order, not outside and above them; it is *the obverse of international obligation*.

That this was the theory most generally held by the founders of our own nation is not open to question.[2] Indeed, it is by analogy to it that the idea was launched that the States of the United States, although bound by the Constitution, were still "sovereign" States. The notion has, moreover, been invoked myriads of times by our Department of State when entering protest against claims or acts of other sovereign governments which it asserted to be unwarranted at International Law. Conversely, our government has at times conceded claims which were urged against it by other governments on the same ground, a notable instance being its acceptance in 1914 of Great Britain's protest, which was based on a certain reading of the Hay-Pauncefote Treaty of 1901, against the exemption of American coastwise shipping from paying tolls for the use of the Panama Canal.[3]

Unfortunately modern International Law also sanctions another concept which ultimately undermines and defeats the concept of a legally limited national sovereignty; I mean the concept of an unlimited right on the part of the members of the Family of Nations to resort to war against one another— a claim which the theory of Total War expands into the right to wage war by any means which appear to promise success. So long as sovereign nations retain by the concession of International Law itself the right to make war upon one another at will the doctrine that national sovereignty is a legally limited sovereignty involves a *felo de se*; the two concepts are mutually unassimilable.

The fact is that the founder of International Law perceived the destructive paradox just pointed out, which he endeavored to remove by elaborating a distinction between "just" and "unjust" wars; and American statesmen and jurists have repeatedly voiced the notion that war is merely *a mode of redress for wrongs at International Law*. These theories, however, have heretofore failed of their intended effect because of the lack of an international organization capable of enforcing the limitations which they imply on the right to make war. But now suppose that the United States should consent to participate in such an organization, could it then be soundly contended that the obligations which it thereby assumed were an infringement upon its "sovereignty"? Such an argument would clearly reject the conception of sovereignty as an attribute which members of the Family of Nations enjoy *under* International Law; and replace it with the conception [(2) above, pages 1-2] that national sovereignty is an inherent, self-bestowed, element of a nation as such, which arises coevally with it and continues unchanged and undiminished so long as the nation continues—which is, in short, the fundamental test of full nationality.

Coming back, then, to conception (2), above, of National Sovereignty, we are compelled to concede at the outset its substantial harmony with nineteenth and early twentieth century juristic concepts, and especially those which are comprised in the so-called Positive, or Austinian, Theory of Law.[4] The notion of *legal* sovereignty—notion (1) on pages 2-3, above—was an outgrowth of the doctrine of Natural Law and Natural Rights, the notion, in Justice Holmes's words, of "a brooding omnipresence in the sky" which bound men in all their relations and whose precepts were addressed to and discoverable by human reason. By the Positive Theory, on the contrary, law is the speech of some definite *human* authority, and the highest human authority is the state, more especially the Nation-State. By this theory all law, from whatever source it may take its *content*, receives its *legality*, its claim to obedience, exclusively from the Nation-State, whence it follows that the legal competence of the Nation-State is limitable only by itself, and the limits thus imposed may be with equal facility cast off.

Several criticisms are prompted. To begin with, as was indicated above, so overvaulting a conception of sovereignty "o'er-leaps itself and falls on t'other side," implying, as it does unavoidably, that a sovereign state is incapable, just because of its sovereignty, of entering into *legally binding* engagements; that in this respect sovereignty, in the sense of capacity to act, is not illimitable but seriously limited. And seeking to avoid this paradox, supporters of the Positive Theory offer a distinction between "legal" and "moral" obligation, conceding the latter to international agreements while denying them the former. The concession is either ineffectual, or it is destructive of the position which it purports to bolster. If it implies that "moral" obligation is less compulsive upon those who are subject to it than "legal" obligation would be, then by so much does a state's sovereignty still impair its capacity for fullest international relationship. If, on the other hand, "moral" obligation is the more compulsive type of obligation, then all talk about "illimitable" sovereignty was meaningless phraseology from the beginning.

Moreover, when we turn from verbal abstractions to the actual history of international intercourse, we find that one of the chief instruments whereby such intercourse has always been furthered in the past has been what the governmental parties to them have undoubtedly regarded as binding engagements, engagements which limited, sometimes drastically, their own immediate freedom of decision and action in promotion of a remoter good. And what has been true in the past will probably continue to be true in the future, a probability which the idea of an international organization for the promotion of peace takes for granted. But the limitation on sovereignty which thus results will, theoretically at least, affect all states alike. It will be reciprocal, and the United States will not find itself at any peculiar disadvantage, a point which is dealt with further when we come to the section on Constitutional v. International Obligation, on page 26.

To sum up: Sovereignty is primarily a logical or verbal concept, or rather it is several such concepts, although wrapped within each of these concepts is a common factual core—that of national independence. When the logical implications of the several theories of sovereignty are closely scrutinized they are found to interpose no obstacle in the way of the participation by the United States in an international organization for the maintenance of international peace. On the contrary, the view of national sovereignty and of its relation to International Law which American statesmen have generally espoused in the past affords a positive argument for such participation, inasmuch as law always implies the existence of *institutions to support the obligations which it imposes.* And when we turn to the central value connoted by the word "sovereignty," national independence, the force of this argument is vastly multiplied, certainly for the great majority of states. But even as regards the United States, powerful nation that it is, what greater compulsion can be imagined than that which is imposed at this moment by our participation in the current war upon the freedom of decision and action of our government and upon our own individual lives? It is indeed impossible to imagine an international organization being seriously proposed for our acceptance whose requirements would amount to any comparable surrender of our actual independence as a community or of our freedom as individuals—a surrender we must always be prepared to renew so long as the unlimited right of states to wage war upon one another remains. *When Total War is the price of Total Sovereignty, the price is too high!*

# II. CONSTITUTIONAL LIMITATIONS

SOVEREIGNTY is a matter of pure theorizing—at any rate, of as pure theorizing as political science is usually able to achieve. Constitutional Limitations, on the contrary, are generally of a hybrid nature. For present purposes we may define the term as comprising rules of a *restrictive* character which the Supreme Court applies to measures of the National Government, and more particularly to acts of Congress, as tests of their conformity with the Constitution of the United States. Supposedly these rules come from the Constitution itself; actually they were frequently imported into the Court's reading of the Constitution from outside speculations. Thus the doctrine of Dual Federalism, which is to be our first concern, in one of its phases contradicts flatly the plain literal sense of relevant provisions of the Constitution. I allude to the once strongly held theory that the "reserved powers" of the States, or an inner core thereof, stand on a level with the constitutional powers of the National Government and hence supply an independent limitation to the latter, notwithstanding the terms of the Supremacy Clause (Article VI, paragraph 2) of the Constitution. Likewise the principle of the Separation of Powers, as it has been applied both by the Court and by the political departments, is greatly indebted to outside theories, beginning with those of "the celebrated Montesquieu," the inventor of the doctrine. In fact, when the subject was broached in the first Congress under the Constitution one or two bolder spirits questioned whether the Constitution recognized the doctrine at all, and certainly it does not do so in explicit terms, offering in that respect a notable contrast to a majority of the State constitutions of the day. On the other hand, when we turn to those provisions of the Constitution which have for their purpose the assurance to private persons of certain rights, like the Bill of Rights, we find that the actual phraseology of the Constitutional Document, given its historical sense, often rules out, or at least renders superfluous, outside conceptions, although in one instance this is conspicuously not the case. I refer to the clause of Amendment V which says that no person shall "be deprived of life, liberty, or property without due process of law." This provision, which was originally intended to assure to accused persons a fair trial, is today construed as authorizing the Supreme Court to pass on the "reasonableness" of the substantive content of legislation—in other words, as endowing the Court with something very like a general veto power; and this result rests altogether on speculative notions which were imported into the Constitution from without.

The fourth, and final, question to be treated in this Chapter is the effect of treaties and acts of Congress when in conflict. The first time it was confronted with this question the Supreme Court unguardedly declared that it "is not settled by the Constitution,"[5] although it is a fundamental, if not *the* fundamental, axiom of Constitutional Law that the Constitution is complete in itself and hence contains an authoritative answer to any question which human ingenuity or the infinite variety of human circumstances can raise respecting its meaning. And that the Court was able to discover suitable materials with which to stop this acknowledged gap in the Constitution, we shall see in due course.

Yet speaking generally, the story that is told here is one of the gradual ironing out of constitutional complexities in this realm of power, that of the National Government to carry on foreign relations. Nor is there any incompatibility between this statement and the one just made regarding constitutional limitations in general, inasmuch as the Court has always in the long run rejected outside views which would *cramp* the National Government's freedom of action in the conduct of its external relations in favor of the other kind. We now turn to a more detailed consideration of Constitutional Limitations.

# A. DUAL FEDERALISM

That the concept of Dual Federalism today interposes no constitutional difficulties in the way of the United States entering into an international organization for the preservation of peace has already been indicated. The subject falls into three parts:

1. While the Constitution attributes to the States a certain rudimentary capacity in the field of foreign relations, it carefully subordinates this capacity to the control of Congress. Article I, Section 10, Paragraph 3 of the Constitution reads: "No State shall, without the consent of Congress, lay any duty of tonnage, keep troops, or ships of war, in time of peace, enter into any agreement or compact with another State, or with a foreign power, or engage in war, unless actually invaded, or in such imminent danger as will not admit of delay."

Commenting in 1840 in the case of *Holmes v. Jennison*[6] on the word "agreement" in this clause, Chief Justice Taney held it to be all-inclusive, and hence to rule out the possibility of a surrender by a State Governor of a fugitive from the justice of a foreign state upon the demand of the government of the latter. He said: "Every part of that instrument [the Constitution] shows that our whole foreign intercourse was intended to be committed to the hands of the general government: and nothing shows it more strongly than the treaty-making power, and the power of appointing and receiving ambassadors; both of which are immediately connected with the question before us, and undoubtedly belong exclusively to the federal government. It was one of the main objects of the Constitution to make us, so far as regarded our foreign relations, one people, and one nation; and to cut off all communications between foreign governments, and the several state authorities. The power now claimed for the states, is utterly incompatible with this evident intention; and would expose us to one of those dangers, against which the framers of the Constitution have so anxiously endeavoured to guard."

These words are the more notable for having been uttered at a period when the doctrine of States Rights stood high in the estimation of the Court and of the country at large; and although the case went off on a question of jurisdiction, the principle here laid down by the Chief Justice, that the power of the National Government in the diplomatic field totally cuts the States off from official contact with the representatives of foreign governments except by the consent of Congress, has never been departed from. It obviously follows that the States enjoy no power in the field of foreign relations which is capable of limiting or in any wise impeding the power of the National Government in the same field.

2. But how is it with the broad powers which concededly do belong to the States over their own internal affairs—their so-called "Police Powers"—are these also without restrictive force on the competence of the National Government to shape the country's policies toward other governments?

The provisions of the Constitution which bear on this question are the Supremacy Clause (Article VI, paragraph 2) and the Tenth Amendment, which, respectively, read as follows:

"This Constitution and the laws of the United States which shall be made in pursuance thereof; and all treaties made, or which shall be made, under the authority of the United States, shall be the supreme law of the land; and the judges in every State shall be bound thereby, anything in the Constitution or laws of any State to the contrary notwithstanding."

"The powers not delegated to the United States by the Constitution, nor prohibited by it to the States, are reserved to the States respectively, or to the people."

It ought to be observed that the Supremacy Clause itself contemplates the retention by the States of certain powers of legislation, but provides at the same time that any exercise by them of such powers which conflicts with the exercise by the National Government of its constitutional powers shall be,

for that reason, constitutionally ineffective; and it was originally assumed that the Tenth Amendment did nothing to
alter the Constitution in this regard. The great leading case is
that of *Ware v. Hylton*,[7] decided in 1796. The facts and
bearing of the case are indicated in the syllabus, which reads
substantially as follows: "A debt due before the war from an
American to a British subject was during the war paid into
the loan office of Virginia in pursuance of a law of that State
of the 20th of December, 1777, sequestering British property
and providing that such payment, and a receipt therefor,
should discharge the debt. 'Held, that the legislature of Virginia,' which 'from the 4th of July, 1776, and before the
Confederation of the United States . . . possessed and exercised all the rights of' an individual government, 'had authority to make such law and that the same was obligatory,' since
'every nation at war with another may confiscate all property
of, including private debts due, the enemy.' 'Such payment
and discharge would' therefore 'be a bar to a subsequent
action, unless the creditor's right was revived by the treaty
of peace,' by which alone 'the restitution, or compensation
for, British property confiscated during the war by any of the
United States,' could be provided for. Held, that the fourth
article of the Treaty of Peace between Great Britain and the
United States of September 3, 1783, nullifies said law of
Virginia, destroys the payment made under it, and revives the
debt, and gives a right of recovery against the principal
debtor, notwithstanding such payment thereof under the
authority of State law."

Elaborating in his opinion on the constitutional problem
involved in the case, Justice Chase wrote: "It seems to me that
treaties made by Congress according to the Confederation,
were superior to the laws of the States; because the Confederation made them obligatory on all the States. . . . But if
doubts could exist before the establishment of the present
national government, they must be entirely removed by the
sixth article of the Constitution which provides 'that all
treaties made or which shall be made under the authority of

the United States, shall be the supreme law of the land.' . . . There can be no limitation on the power of the people of the United States. By their authority the State constitutions were made, and by their authority the Constitution of the United States was established; and they had the power to change or abolish the State constitutions, or to make them yield to the General Government and to treaties made by their authority. . . . It is the declared will of the people of the United States that every treaty made, by the authority of the United States, shall be superior to the constitution and laws of any individual State; and their will alone is to decide. . . ."[8]

The sweeping doctrine laid down in these words was maintained without retraction or modification by the Court under Chief Justice Marshall. The type of treaty provision which most frequently raised the constitutional issue during this period was the concession by the United States, in return for a like concession by the other contracting power, of the right of citizens or subjects of the latter to hold real property in the United States, a provision which often conflicted with State legislation or State common law. Such treaty provisions were invariably sustained by the Court on the principle that since such stipulations were incontrovertibly within the treaty-making power, they were supreme law of the land, anything in State law to the contrary notwithstanding.[9]

In the period following upon Marshall's death, however, a new point of view emerged in our Constitutional Law, one which found clear expression for the first time in 1837 in the Court's opinion in *New York v. Miln*.[10] In that case a New York statute laying certain requirements upon captains of vessels entering New York harbor with alien passengers was involved. Speaking for the Court, Justice Barbour said:

"There is, then, no collision between the law in question, and the acts of Congress just commented on; and therefore, if the State law were to be considered as partaking of the nature of a commercial regulation it would stand the test of the most rigid scrutiny, if tried by the standard laid down in the reasoning of the Court, quoted from the case of *Gibbons v. Ogden*.

"But we do not place our opinion on this ground. We choose rather to plant ourselves on what we consider impregnable positions. They are these: That a State has the same undeniable and unlimited jurisdiction over all persons and things, within its territorial limits, as any foreign nation; where that jurisdiction is not surrendered or restrained by the Constitution of the United States. That, by virtue of this, it is not only the right, but the bounden and solemn duty of a State, to advance the safety, happiness and prosperity of its people, and to provide for its general welfare, by any and every act of legislation, which it may deem to be conducive to these ends; where the power over the particular subject, or the manner of its exercise is not surrendered or restrained, in the manner just stated. That all those powers which relate to merely municipal legislation, or what may, perhaps, more properly be called internal police, are not thus surrendered or restrained; and that, consequently, in relation to these, the authority of a State is complete, unqualified and exclusive."[11]

That is to say, the police powers of the States constitute a reserve of *exclusive* powers, with the result that any subject-matter which falls within their jurisdiction is, *for that reason,* outside the ambit of any national power whatsoever. The primary source of this new doctrine were certain fears of the slave-holding interest, fear particularly of the power of Congress over interstate commerce and, later, its power over the territories of the United States. But inevitably the same doctrine came in the course of time to color also the Court's conception of the relation of the treaty-making power to the reserved powers of the States. Thus in a case decided in 1856, in which plaintiff disputed the right of the State of Louisiana under the Treaty of 1853 with France, to impose a succession tax upon property inherited prior to the treaty, the Court, speaking by Chief Justice Taney, said: "If the property vested in him at the time, it could vest only in the manner, upon the conditions, authorized by the laws of the State. . . . And certainly a treaty, subsequently [i.e. to the vesting of the property] made by the United States with France could not devest rights of property already vested in the State, even if the words of the treaty had imported such intention. But the words of the article . . . clearly apply to cases happening afterwards."[12]

And four years later counsel for defendant State argued similarly: "The United States had no power by treaty to interfere with or control the right of the State of Louisiana to tax property within its limits or regulate the descent of property in the State," these powers not having been surrendered by the States. But once again the Court evaded the constitutional issue by ruling that the treaty did not apply to the situation before it, although in language sufficiently ominous. It has been suggested, Justice Campbell recited, "That the Government of the United States is incompetent to regulate testamentary dispositions or laws of inheritance of foreigners in reference to property within the States. The question is one of great magnitude, but it is not important in the decision of this cause and we consequently abstain from entering upon its consideration."[13]

Save, therefore, as a *narrowing* principle of treaty interpretation, the doctrine that State power comprises an independent limitation on the powers of the National Government does not appear to have entered the diplomatic field, and even in that regard it was discarded by the Court in 1879 in the case of *Hauenstein v. Lynham*.[14] In this case the Court upheld the right of a citizen of the Swiss Republic under the Treaty of 1850 with that country to recover the estate of a relative dying intestate in Virginia, to sell the same, and to send the proceeds from the sale out of the country. The opinion of Justice Swayne for the unanimous Court contains a vague expression to the effect that "there are doubtless limitations to this power as there are to all others arising under such instruments" as the Constitution of the United States, but this circumstance does not detract from the opinion's thoroughly satisfactory character as a reiteration of the early constitutional doctrine in this class of cases, to the operation of which it accords the fullest scope. Thus with reference to the early case of *Fairfax v. Hunter*,[15] Justice Swayne adopts Justice

Cushing's opinion that "it is the direct constitutional question in its fullest conditions." Again he states that it is admitted on all hands that "if the treaty applies, its efficacy must necessarily be complete." Finally, again leaning upon the earlier case, he urges this consideration: "If the National Government has not the power to do what is done by such treaties, it cannot be done at all, for the States are expressly forbidden to enter into treaties."

Two recent cases emphasize and amplify these results. In *Missouri v. Holland*,[16] decided in 1920, the Court sustained a treaty with Great Britain and implementing legislation by Congress whereby game birds seasonally migrating from Canada into this country were brought under the protection of the United States, in face of the conceded proposition that the protection of such birds had hitherto fallen exclusively to the "quasi-sovereign" powers of the States. Speaking for the Court, Justice Holmes rejected the idea that the treaty-making power was limited by "some invisible radiation from the general terms of the Tenth Amendment," and asserted that the fact that the treaty dealt with a matter of national interest was enough to bring it within "the authority of the United States" in the sense of the Supremacy Clause. And he added, "it is not lightly to be assumed that, in matters requiring national action, 'a power which must belong to and somewhere reside in every civilized government' is not to be found."

The other case just alluded to is *University of Illinois v. United States*,[17] in which in 1933 it was ruled that the States and their instrumentalities were not free to import articles without paying the duties imposed by the Tariff Act of 1922. "The principle of duality in our system of government," said Chief Justice Hughes for the Court, "does not touch the authority of Congress in the regulation of foreign commerce." "To permit the States and their instrumentalities to import commodities for their own use, regardless of the requirements imposed by the Congress, would undermine, if not destroy, the single control which it was one of the dominant purposes of the Constitution to create."[18]

The dual federal principle, therefore, does not limit in any way the power of the National Government in treaty-making or in the governance of foreign commerce, the operation of the Supremacy Clause being as regards these powers complete and unqualified. Indeed, the important decision of the Court in *United States v. Darby*[19] two years ago treats the same principle as today applying to any and every exertion of national legislative power against which the only constitutional objection urged is that it invades the historical province of the States. The measure before the Court on that occasion was the Fair Labor Standards Act of 1938 which, in an effort to close the channels of interstate commerce to goods not produced in accordance with the standards set by the act, makes it a misdemeanor against the United States to *produce* goods "intended" for such commerce except in accordance with these standards. This feature of the act was especially attacked as trespassing upon "the exclusive powers of the States over production," an idea to which the Court itself had subscribed many times over in the recent past. Chief Justice Stone, nevertheless, speaking for the Court, repelled the contention, holding the section in question to be a "necessary and proper" provision for the effective carrying out of the main purposes of the measure, the prevention of the spread of substandard labor conditions through interstate competition; and the notion that the Tenth Amendment was capable of affecting the issue in any respect he rejected peremptorily.

3. The last element of the concept of Dual Federalism to demand attention is the doctrine that the National Government is "a government of enumerated powers only," and consequently under the necessity at all times of justifying its measures juridically by pointing to some particular clause or clauses of the Constitution which, when read separately or in combination, may be thought to grant power adequate to such measures. In spite of such recent decisions as that in

*United States v. Darby* this time-honored doctrine still guides the authoritative interpreters of the Constitution in determining the validity of acts which are passed by Congress in presumed exercise of its powers of *domestic* legislation—the course of reasoning pursued by the Chief Justice in the Darby Case itself is proof that such is the fact. In the field of *foreign relations,* on the contrary, the doctrine of Enumerated Powers has always had a difficult row to hoe, and today may be unqualifiedly asserted to be defunct.

In the number of the *Federalist* in which he deals with the War Power of the proposed National Government, Hamilton treats it as comprising a mosaic of certain specific powers; and by parity of reasoning the entire competence of the National Government in the sphere of international relationship would have to be regarded as resting on specific, enumerated powers or on combinations thereof.[20] Indeed, as late as 1917 we find former Chief Justice Hughes adopting the same approach in a public address entitled, significantly, "War Powers Under the Constitution."[21] Yet Hamilton in 1787 and Mr. Hughes 132 years afterward were both at pains to assure us that the mosaic of specific powers which they adduced would always prove equal to any and all exigencies of national defense; or, to generalize their argument, would be equal to all exigencies of international relationship. Obviously the assumed coherency of these two positions—that the National Government enjoys only *enumerated,* yet always *sufficient,* powers to deal with other governments—takes something for granted—a fact which was sensed at an early date.

In the old case of *Penhallow v. Doane,*[22] which was decided by the Supreme Court in 1795, certain counsel thought it pertinent to urge the following conception of the War Power: "A formal compact is not essential to the institution of a government. Every nation that governs itself, under what form soever, without any dependence on a foreign power, is a sovereign state. In every society there must be a sovereignty. 1 Dall. Rep. 46, 57. Vatt. B. 1. ch. 1. sec. 4. The powers of war form an inherent characteristic of national sovereignty;

and, it is not denied, that Congress possessed those powers. . . ."[23]

To be sure, only two of the Justices felt it necessary to comment on this argument, which one of them endorsed, while
the other rejected it. Yet seventy-five years later Justice
Bradley incorporated closely kindred doctrine into his con-
curring opinion in the *Legal Tender Cases;*[24] and in the years
following the Court itself frequently brought the same general
outlook to questions affecting the National Government's
powers in the field of foreign relations. Thus in the *Chinese
Exclusion Case,*[25] decided in 1889, Justice Field in asserting
the unlimited power of the National Government, and hence
of Congress, to exclude aliens from American shores, re-
marked: "While under our Constitution and form of government the great mass of local matters is controlled by local
authorities, the United States, in their relation to foreign
countries and their subjects or citizens, are one nation, in-
vested with the powers which belong to independent nations,
the exercise of which can be invoked for the maintenance of
its absolute independence and security throughout its entire
territory."[26]

And four years later the power of the National Government
to deport alien residents at the option of Congress was based
by Justice Gray on the same general ground, in these words:
"The United States are a sovereign and independent nation,
and are vested by the Constitution with the entire control of
international relations, and with all the powers of government
necessary to maintain that control and make it effective. The
only government of this country, which other nations recognize or treat with, is the Government of the Union; and the
only American flag known throughout the world is the flag
of the United States."[27]

Finally, in 1936, Justice Sutherland, speaking for the Court
in *United States v. Curtiss-Wright Corporation,*[28] took over
bodily counsel's argument of 140 years earlier, and elevated it
to the head of the column of authoritative constitutional doctrine. His words were as follows: "A political society cannot

endure without a supreme will somewhere. Sovereignty is never held in suspense. When, therefore, the external sovereignty of Great Britain in respect to the colonies ceased, it immediately passed to the Union. . . .

"It results that the investment of the Federal government with the powers of external sovereignty did not depend upon the affirmative grants of the Constitution. The powers to declare and wage war, to conclude peace, to make treaties, to maintain diplomatic relations with other sovereignties, if they had never been mentioned in the Constitution, would have vested in the Federal government as a necessary concomitant of nationality."[29]

In short, the power of the National Government in the field of international relationship is not a complexus of particular enumerated powers, but is an *inherent power, one which is attributed to the National Government on the ground solely of its belonging to the American People as a sovereign political entity at International Law. It follows that silence on the part of the Constitution as to the power of the National Government to adopt any particular measure in relation to other nations is not a denial of such power, as it would be if the doctrine of Enumerated Powers applied, but is, on the contrary, an affirmance of power.*

At this point it may occur to the reader to suggest that the above discussion is unnecessarily elaborate, that it would have sufficed for my purpose to have shown merely that the 'treaty-making power* is of indefinite scope and unhampered by the reserved powers of the States. The answer to this criticism is twofold. As a matter of history the notion of the indefinite scope of the treaty-making power is itself reflective of the concept of the National Government's plenary powers in the field of foreign relations and was not always conceded in earlier days. Indeed, the argument was even offered that the treaty-making power was not a substantive power at all, but merely a method whereby the National Government was authorized to exercise certain of its enumerated powers, its power to regulate foreign commerce for instance.[30] And as we have just

[ 19 ]

seen, theory regarding the scope of the treaty power *vis-à-vis* the powers of the States fluctuated considerably prior to the Civil War. Of far greater importance, however, is the second answer to the above criticism, which is that if the treaty-making authority is the *only* constitutional way the United States may today take into an international organization for the promotion of peace, *if the legislative competence of Congress does not afford a possible alternative route*, then the nation may find its road blocked, its expectations frustrated. Furthermore, once the United States is participant in an international organization, the powers which the National Government will find it requisite to call into operation through Congress, in order to discharge its obligations efficiently and continuously, will be of indefinite range. Both of these points are further elucidated below.

## B. SEPARATION OF POWERS

The second great structural principle of the National Government is supplied by the Montesquieuan doctrine of the Separation of Powers, namely, that there are three fundamentally distinct "powers" of government, the Executive, the Legislative, and the Judicial, each of which ought to be lodged in a distinct department of government.[81] Although the extent to which this doctrine is actually recognized in the Constitution of the United States has been the subject of frequent controversy,[32] we are here concerned only with its effect on the conduct of American foreign relations.

Regarded as a principle of constitutional interpretation the doctrine naturally prompts an effort to define "the three powers" by assigning to each a more or less distinctive content and method, and by claiming for the respective bearers of the powers thus identified a certain degree of autonomy in their exercise. But as we shall see, operation of the doctrine has been very different as regards "judicial power" on the one hand and "executive power" on the other, yet with the net result in each instance of relaxing constitutional limitations in the foreign field.

1. To consider "judicial power" first—Montesquieu's dictum that this power of government is "next to nothing" certainly comes close to literal realization in the diplomatic sphere. It is true, as some of the cases reviewed above serve to demonstrate, that American courts are occasionally called upon to give recognition and enforcement to private claims which purport to be based on a treaty or some other international engagement to which the United States is party. But not only are the provisions or stipulations thus invoked subject at all times to repeal by Congress as "law of the land" which the courts are entitled to notice and enforce,[33] but whenever claims of this nature are advanced in reliance on contentious views concerning the obligation of the National Government *to the other contracting government,* the courts deem it to be a corollary of the principle of the Separation of Powers that they must adopt any clearly indicated views of Congress and/or the President, the so-called "Political Departments." This doctrine, termed the doctrine of Political Questions, was first announced by Chief Justice Marshall in 1829 in the case of *Foster v. Neilson.*[34] The question immediately at issue there was the validity of a grant made by the Spanish government in 1804 of land lying to the east of the Mississippi River, and involved in this question was the further one whether the region between the Perdido and Mississippi Rivers belonged in 1804 to Spain or the United States. Marshall held that the Court was bound by the action of the political departments, the President and Congress, in claiming the land for the United States. He said:

"If those departments which are entrusted with the foreign intercourse of the nation, which assert and maintain its interests against foreign powers, have unequivocally asserted its right of dominion over a country of which it is in possession, and which it claims under a treaty; if the legislature has acted on the construction thus asserted, it is not in its own courts that this construction is to be denied. A question like this respecting the boundaries of nations is, as has been truly said, more a political than a legal question, and in its discussion, the courts of every country must respect the pronounced will of the legislature."[35]

The view thus stated has been reiterated by the Court many times.[36]

2. Of more immediate pertinence, however, to the present investigation is the operation of the doctrine of the Separation of Powers as a constructive principle on the opening clause of Article II of the Constitution, which reads, "The executive power shall be vested in a President of the United States of America."[37] For it is altogether evident that the entrance of the United States into an international organization must depend in the first instance on the leadership which the President is constitutionally able to bring to such an enterprise.

The event which gave the constitutional twig its initial bent in this regard occurred in connection with President Washington's issuance early in 1793 of a proclamation of neutrality on the outbreak of war between France and Great Britain. Since no clause of the Constitution specifically authorized the President to take such a step, the validity of the proclamation was immediately challenged, with the result of precipitating a newspaper discussion between Hamilton writing as "Pacificus" and Madison writing as "Helvidius" the fame of which has endured to this day.[38] Hamilton's defense of the proclamation rested on the contention that the conduct of foreign relations was inherently an "executive" function, and hence was lodged by the above quoted clause in the President alone except as the Constitution might in more definite terms provide otherwise, the participation of the Senate in treaty-making and the power of Congress to declare war being examples. Madison's answer was that the latter exception determined the issue, since it proved the intention of the Constitution to lodge in Congress the power of ultimate decision as to American foreign policy. In fact, he continued, the President's only exclusive power in this field was the power to receive foreign representatives, a merely "ceremonial" power which he was under constitutional obligation to employ for the purpose of forwarding Congress's decisions. Madison charged, indeed, that Hamilton's argument was nothing more nor less than a brazen attempt to foist upon the Constitution the prerogatives of the British King, the very thing which the Philadelphia Convention had thought to forestall by the war-declaring provision.

Alluding to the debate between "Pacificus" and "Helvidius" some forty years afterwards, John Quincy Adams paid tribute to the latter's subtlety and ingenuity, but concluded, nonetheless, that "Pacificus" had proved the better prophet, that the attempt of the Constitution to lodge the power to declare war in Congress was an "error," but an error which actual practice under the Constitution had effectually corrected.[39] The circumstances surrounding the outbreak of war with Mexico less than a decade later dramatically reinforced Adams's verdict, and since then the American people have fought three great wars which were the direct, even if not the calculated, outcome of Presidential policies. For as a *fait accompli* war is absolutely compulsive; there is nothing that the other organs of government can do about it save to accept it and take measures accordingly. It automatically creates a public opinion which, at least so long as victory is doubtful, coerces the Legislative organ to dance to the tunes called by the Executive organ.

3. There is one further aspect of the principle of the Separation of Powers which it is pertinent to mention in this connection. I mean the corollary maxim, hailing from Locke's *Second Treatise on Government*, that "the legislative cannot transfer the power of making laws to any other hands."[40] For of what use is it to separate powers constitutionally if their official trustees may at any time remerge them? In the field of domestic legislation the Lockian maxim, although it is drawn out rather thin in certain recent cases,[41] still survives in theory. In the field of foreign relations, by the decision in 1936 in *United States v. Curtiss-Wright Corporation*,[42] it is very much otherwise. There, as Justice Sutherland

points out, the indefinite powers of Congress stand alongside of the "cognate" and often overlapping powers of the President, while by the ruling of the case, both categories of power may be united in the hands of the President whenever Congress chooses to authorize the mergence. The holding is thoroughly accordant with the doctrine of Political Questions and testifies, like that doctrine, to the settled reluctance of the Court to thrust its oar into the turbulent waters of foreign policy-making.

## C. PRIVATE RIGHTS

While, as we have just seen, the National Government has today become to all intents and purposes a centralized government in the sphere of foreign relations, it still remains nevertheless a government *all* of whose powers are confronted by the Constitution with certain stipulated safeguards in behalf of private rights. Thus Congress is forbidden to pass any *ex post facto* laws or bills of attainder, and the National Government is in general forbidden to take private property "for public use without just compensation," or to deprive persons "of life, liberty or property without due process of law"; or to try persons charged with serious offenses against the United States except by certain prescribed procedures, and so on and so forth.[43] Do these provisions limit the powers of the National Government in the conduct of foreign relations? Inasmuch as it has been repeatedly held that they limit even the war power of the National Government, at least when rights of citizens of the United States are involved, the question just put must undoubtedly be answered with a general affirmative, a conclusion which is reinforced by numerous dicta to like effect with respect to the treaty-making power.[44]

Indeed, it may be plausibly argued that specific constitutional provisions in favor of private rights are logically more compelling as against a general, indefinite power than as against definite, enumerated powers, which may be thought to mark a considered surrender of rights falling within their orbit. Despite all which, objections to treaty-provisions and other international engagements of the United States which were based on the ground that they invaded private rights have been few and far between, and have been, moreover, thus far consistently repelled by the Court.

The pioneer case is *Ware v. Hylton*,[45] which was mentioned on an earlier page for its bearing on the subject of the relation of the treaty power and the reserved powers of the States. Here it was held that a debt which had been owing at the outbreak of the Revolution from a resident of Virginia to a British subject, and had been discharged in the course of the war by payment under a Virginia statute into the State treasury, had been revived by Article IV of the Treaty of 1783, and hence was still collectible by the original creditor or his assignees. Conceding that under "immutable principles of justice" the twice-mulcted debtor ought to be compensated, Justice Chase asserted, nonetheless, that Congress "had the power to sacrifice the rights and interests of private citizens to secure the safety and prosperity of the public,"[46] while Justices Paterson, Wilson, and Cushing did not so much as advert to the hardship put upon the American debtor. Nor does the circumstance that the treaty was made by the Congress of the Confederation appear to be a material element of the holding, inasmuch as all of the Justices assumed that its force and effect in 1796 proceeded immediately from the Supremacy Clause of the Constitution.

A modern counterpart to *Ware v. Hylton* is provided by the Russian Insurance Cases, of which *U.S. v. Pink*,[47] decided early in 1942, seems to be the final and determinative one. Here it was ruled that the "executive agreement" under which our government extended recognition to the Soviet government and entered into diplomatic relations with it in 1933 required recognition and enforcement from all American courts, State as well as national, of the Soviet government's decrees of confiscation with respect to the assets in the United States of certain Russian insurance companies, and that the claims against such companies of foreign creditors in the United States were superseded under the agreement by certain claims of American citizens and the government of the United States itself against the Russian government; and this result was reached in face of the concession that "aliens as well as citizens are entitled to the protection of the Fifth Amendment." Chief Justice Stone filed a dissenting opinion for himself and Justice Roberts in which he challenged the majority's construction of the executive agreement, but without challenging its constitutionality as construed. "Even though," said he, "the two governments might have stipulated for alteration by this Government of its municipal law, and the consequent surrender of the rights of individuals," still such an intention ought to be clearly expressed and not rest on mere inference.[48]

The subject need not be canvassed further. In contrast to the alleged rights of the States, the constitutional immunities of the citizen have not, in general, fallen athwart the pathway of American foreign policy, nor are they likely to do so in the future. But this will be due, as it has been due in the past, much less to the direct operation of the Constitution than to the historic attitude of American public men toward such immunities. The limitation is an "internal" rather than an "external" one.

## D. CONSTITUTIONAL *V.* INTERNATIONAL OBLIGATION

The last question to arise under the general heading of "Constitutional Limitations" may be restated thus: Does the Constitution contain or imply any principle which makes it impossible for the National Government to enter validly into a general engagement with other governments either to exercise its constitutional powers in the furtherance of international peace, or to forego their exercise for the same purpose? As we saw earlier, no such proposition can be conceded in deference to the general principle of National Sovereignty, otherwise the United States would be in the paradoxical situation of being at once more and less sovereign than, for example, Great Britain or the U.S.S.R. The question now before us is whether the Constitution of the United States, nevertheless, requires such a concession.

Underlying this question is a fundamental assumption without whose support the question lacks logical coherence. This is the belief that a *constitutional* obligation attaches to and sanctions the *international* obligation of any treaty and, by parity of reasoning, any international agreement to which the United States is party. Is this assumption sound?

The literary source of the assumption is furnished by memoranda which Alexander Hamilton prepared for President Washington in 1796, when the House of Representatives, in the course of considering an appropriation for carrying the Jay Treaty into effect, requested the President to send it a copy of Jay's instructions. Denying that the House had the right to ask for the document in question, or indeed to pass upon the merits of the treaty in any respect, Hamilton argued in effect as follows: "That the Constitution empowered the President and Senate to make treaties; that to make a treaty as between nations meant to conclude a contract obligatory on their good faith; that a contract could not be obligatory to the validity of which the assent of another body was constitutionally necessary; that the Constitution declared a treaty made under the authority of the United States to be a supreme law, but that that could not be a supreme law to the validity of which the assent of another body in the state was constitutionally necessary; . . . 'Hence it follows,' he said, 'that the House of Representatives have no moral power to refuse the execution of a treaty which is not contrary to the Constitution, because it pledges the public faith; and have no legal power to refuse its execution because it is a law—until at least it ceases to be a law by a regular act of revocation of the competent authority.' "[49]

Notwithstanding the approval which it has at times received from publicists,[50] Hamilton's theory has not in fact prevailed. In later years Attorneys General were frequently called upon to instruct the President as to his duty when an act of Congress conflicted with an earlier treaty, and invariably answered that the rule of later date was the valid rule;[51] and in the *Head Money Cases*,[52] decided in 1884, and the *Chinese Exclusion Case*[53] decided in 1889, the Supreme Court adopted this doctrine as binding on itself in an analogous situation. Admitting in the latter case that an act passed by Congress in 1888 was in flat contravention of express stipulations of the treaty of 1868 with the Emperor of China, Justice Field, speaking for the Court, said: "It is not on that account invalid or to be restricted in its enforcement. The treaties were of no greater legal obligation than the act of Congress. By the Constitution, laws made in pursuance thereof and treaties made under the authority of the United States are both declared to be the supreme law of the land, and no paramount authority is given to one over the other. A treaty, it is true, is in its nature a contract between nations and is often merely promissory in its character, requiring legislation to carry its stipulations into effect. Such legislation will be open to future repeal or amendment. If the treaty operates by its own force, and relates to a subject within the power of Congress, it can be deemed in that particular only the equivalent of a legislative act, to be repealed or modified at the pleasure of Congress. In either case the last expression of the sovereign will must control."[54]

In short, *a treaty is not vested with the supremacy of the Constitution,* as Hamilton had asserted, *but stands constitutionally on a level with an act of Congress of even date and is, consequently, subject to repeal, just as the latter is, by a later act of Congress.* But this is far from signifying, on the other hand, that an act of Congress which, by intention or otherwise, repeals a treaty provision concludes the rights at *International Law* of the other party to the treaty. Dealing with this point in the *Head Money Cases,* Justice Miller wrote: "A treaty is primarily an international compact between independent nations," and depends for its enforcement "on the interest and power of the governments which are parties to it. If these fail its infraction becomes the subject of international negotiations and reclamations" by the disadvantaged state, "which may in the end be enforced by actual war."[55]

Thus, *international obligation is one thing, constitutional obligation a different thing.* When it is a question of the former the United States is just as much entitled to determine the extent of its rights and duties at International Law as any other sovereign state is, *and not a whit more*; a situation which the Constitution alters in no wise. Or to state the point in different words, *in relation to the international engagements of the United States Congress stands on precisely the same footing as does Parliament, for instance, in relation to the international engagements of Great Britain.* The answer to the above question is, therefore, no.

To sum up the argument of this Chapter: The concept of Dual Federalism, a fundamental ingredient between 1837 and 1937 of constitutional interpretation affecting national power in the domestic forum, is of no importance whatever in the sphere of international relations—in this sphere the government of the United States is a government of centralized, plenary power, in the exercise whereof it is in no respect limited by the coexistence of the States or by their acknowledged powers. Likewise, the principle of the Separation of Powers has been read out of the Constitution as a factor capable of embarrassing the conduct of the foreign relations of the United States. In fact, by the stimulus which it early imparted to sweeping conceptions of the "executive power" of the President in the international field, the principle has wrought to exactly the opposite effect. Nor again are the provisions of the Constitution in protection of private rights likely to present substantial difficulties to any project for an international organization which American statesmen would sponsor even though those provisions were to be stricken from the Constitution. Finally, the Constitution in nowise impairs the constitutional power of the National Government to accept limitations on its freedom of action in support of international peace, for such limitations will derive their force and effect exclusively from the principles of international justice, honor, and good will, *and from that species of political wisdom which prefers the long view to the short view*; not at all from the Constitution or to any other political institutions which are peculiar to the United States.

In a word, *the question whether the United States should enter an international organization* for the promotion of peace and of what pledges it should give with respect to the use of its constitutional powers to the same end, *is one which the appropriate agencies of the National Government are free to decide on grounds of national interest, substantially unfettered by Constitutional Limitations of any kind.*

# III. THE SENATE AND TREATIES

·From Constitutional Limitations we turn to a matter of *constitutional structure*. The two things are sometimes more alike than might at first glance appear. Constitutional limitations on power *can* be very flexible; as we have seen, they *are* very flexible in the realm of foreign relations. But they can also be very stiff; while the constitutional clauses which provide the mechanisms whereby power is exercised are quite commonly couched in terms that admit of little or no interpretation. The result is that if a particular, highly essential mechanism of the Constitution becomes unworkable for the purpose it was intended to serve, then either the constitutional structure must put forth, by the processes of constitutional amendment or otherwise, another mechanism adapted to the same purpose, or hope of action, however essential action may be, must be abandoned. In the end, a defective or atrophied constitutional structure may prove to be the most constrictive kind of constitutional limitation.

Article II, section 2, paragraph 2, of the Constitution reads: "He [the President] shall have power, by and with the advice and consent of the Senate, to make treaties, provided two-thirds of the Senators present concur." How serious a constitutional obstacle does the role of the Senate in treaty-making today interpose to entrance by the United States into an international organization for the maintenance of international peace?

On premises previously set forth the United States is constitutionally competent to enter into any type of agreement whatsoever with any other nation which is similarly competent. At the same time, Constitutional Law and practice have long since come to support a distinction between "treaties" and less formal "agreements." Indeed, this distinction is reflected in the Constitution itself, Article I, section 10 of which forbids the States absolutely to "enter into any treaty, alliance or confederation," but merely limits their entering "into any agreement or compact with another State, or with a foreign power" by the requirement that they first obtain the consent of Congress. But this distinction in nowise restricts the scope of the treaty-making power, for the record of constitutional practice makes it clear that any agreement with a foreign government in the making of which the advice and consent of the Senate is sought is, for that reason if no other, a "treaty" in the sense of Article II, section 2, paragraph 2. The sole importance which the distinction in question retains today arises from the support which it lends to the position that there are types of international agreement into which the United States cannot constitutionally enter *except* by the treaty-making route as laid down in Article II, section 2.

The classic demonstration that the two-thirds rule interposes an almost insuperable obstacle to entrance by the United States into an international organization is generally thought to be afforded by the fate of the League of Nations Covenant in 1920. What is generally overlooked with regard to this famous struggle between the President and the Senate is that it was the natural, if not inevitable, outcome of 120 years of institutional development. That personal factors were also important may be granted, but their importance would certainly have been much less except for the leverage which the previous evolution of the treaty-making authority afforded them, involving as this did increasing differentiation of function as between the authority's constituent organs.

Under the Articles of Confederation, the single-chambered Congress, in which each State had one vote, was empowered to conclude treaties by the favorable vote of nine of thirteen States;[56] and in the provision originally offered on the subject to the Philadelphia Convention the Senate succeeded to this power.[57] Not until September 7, ten days before its final adjournment, did the Convention adopt the existing provision, incidentally rejecting by a vote of ten States to one a proposal by Wilson of Pennsylvania that treaties should be made by the President with the advice and consent of the Senate and House of Representatives.[58]

Why was the Senate thus preferred to the House and why was the two-thirds requirement retained after the President was finally brought into the picture? There were several reasons. One was the persuasion that the more numerous House would be incapable of the secrecy which is supposed to be requisite in treaty-making whereas the Senate would, a theory which has scarcely been verified by events. And since the Senate alone could be utilized for the business, then a two-thirds vote of its membership was required both because there were vital sectional interests to be protected and because treaties were to be "law of the land" in addition to being international agreements. Finally, it is probable that the strong contingent which had been trying unsuccessfully throughout the Convention to load the President with a council akin to those which existed to curb executive power in most of the State constitutions, staked their last throw on the idea that the Senate could be made to discharge a kindred function in the proposed National Government.[59]

Unfortunately, the theory that the Senate could be made to serve the President as a council in the diplomatic field broke down the first time it was put to the test, being in fact rejected by the Senate itself. This was when President Washington, on August 22, 1789, went in person to the Senate chamber to consult it about some proposed treaties with the Southern Indians. Instead of answering the questions which the President put to them, the Senators present referred them to a committee. "This," exclaimed the President heatedly, "defeats every purpose of my coming here," and although, according to a witness of the scene, he "cooled down by degrees," he seems never to have repeated the experiment of oral consultation.[60] Indeed, the successive steps by which the famous Jay Treaty was concluded for the United States six years later demarcate already the part of the President in treaty-making from that of the Senate along virtually the line that still holds.

The treaty was negotiated in London under instructions in the framing of which the Senate had no hand, and when it was laid before that body the latter, instead of rejecting or accepting it outright, as it would have a nomination to office, proceeded in effect to amend it as if it had been a legislative project; nor did the Administration challenge the Senate's right to pursue this course, although the British government was at first disposed to do so.[61] In a word, *by the action of the Senate itself its character as an executive council was from the very beginning put on the way to absorption into its more usual character as a legislative chamber*, a decision which subsequent developments put in time beyond all possibility of recall.

One such development was the creation by Washington early in 1793 of what soon came to be called "the Cabinet" out of the heads of the chief executive departments to advise him as to the diplomatic crisis occasioned by the outbreak of war between France and Great Britain.[62] Another was the increase in the membership of the Senate between 1789 and 1795 from twenty-two to thirty-two members, thus foreshadowing a body too numerous to trust safely with some kinds of state secrets and too unwieldy for intimate consultation. Yet not till 1816 did the Senate, by setting up the standing Committee on Foreign Relations, formally recognize the realities of the situation which both its increasing size and its predominantly legislative role created;[63] and even then it still clung to the "executive session" in the consideration of treaties until the fight over the Treaty of Versailles, when this last vestige of its character as a council was ruthlessly sacrificed to its character as a chamber of unlimited debate. And it is the latter character which Senator Connally invoked a few weeks ago in an attempt to justify the evident purpose of the Committee on Foreign Relations to administer to the Fulbright Resolution the treatment it had already dealt out to the Ball-Burton, Hatch-Hill, the so-called "$B_2H_2$ Resolution."[64] Among other things Mr. Connally said:

"The Committee on Foreign Relations does not desire at

this particular moment to afford opportunity for intemperate and trouble-making debate on the floor of the Senate. It is known to all well-informed men that the utmost freedom of debate is permitted under the Senate rules.

"It is further known that Senators do not hesitate to avail themselves of that unlimited freedom. International relations are delicate and sensitive. Unity and harmony require consultation and cooperation. We cannot perform the task alone."[65]

The Senator casts a nostalgic glance to a past which was never a present, a time when the Senate felt and behaved as an executive council should. Can the leopard, which Scripture assures us "cannot change its spots," change them back again? Even "the greatest legislative assembly on earth" might well confess itself unequal to such a miracle.

It is true that Presidents bent on shifting a dangerous responsibility have sometimes recollected opportunely that there is "safety in a multitude of counsellors." The outstanding instance is that of Polk, who in 1846, fearing that his campaign pledge of "fifty-four forty, or fight," respecting the Oregon boundary dispute with Great Britain, might interfere with his more extensive designs on Mexico, sought and obtained from the Senate its preliminary approval of an offer to Great Britain, which the latter accepted, of a compromise boundary at 49°. And even as late as 1908 Woodrow Wilson, after noting that there could be little doubt that the Convention of 1787 intended that the Senate should advise the President as to appointments and treaties "in the spirit of an executive council associated with him upon terms of confidential cooperation," declared that on this premise it was still not only the President's privilege, but his best policy and plain duty to deal with the Upper Chamber on that footing. He then added: "If he have character, modesty, devotion, and insight as well as force, he can bring the contending elements of the system together into a great and efficient body of common counsel."[66] How far Mr. Wilson himself came from realizing this perhaps impossible ideal in his own relations with the Senate is a matter of agreed history.

The failure of the United States to enter the League of Nations in 1919-1920 was due therefore only in part to the two-thirds rule which the Constitution lays down for Senate approval of treaties. Much more largely it was due to the operation of that rule in a situation which the Framers of the Constitution had not anticipated and for which the two-thirds rule was not designed. *The wording of the Constitution itself visualizes treaty-making as one continuous process to be performed by a single authority, the President acting throughout in consultation with the Senate. From the first, however, the Senate insisted upon asserting its independence of identity in the treaty-making business, thereby splitting the constitutional authority into two authorities, performing separate differentiated functions, a Presidential function of formulation and negotiation followed by a Senatorial function—completely legislative in character and motivation—of criticism and amendment, or of criticism and rejection.* And subsequent events have only confirmed this divorcement—unattended by any obligation of support on either side—into two often politically antagonistic organs. In short, the two-thirds rule was an anomaly before it was ever put into operation, and everything that has happened since 1789 both within the constitutional system and outside of it has contributed to aggravate its abnormity.

The question arises, consequently, whether there is any way of constitutionally obviating the potential difficulty which the two-thirds rule today opposes to entrance by the United States into an international organization. That the difficulty might be validly removed by constitutional amendment is of course evident. Only recently the *New York Times* urged editorially that if an amendment empowering the President to conclude treaties subject to the approval of a legislative majority in the two houses were to be presently submitted to conventions in the States, its ratification by the required three-fourths of the States would in all probability be forthcoming before the end of the current war.[67] Not only does the "if" in this suggestion brush aside entirely too casually the supreme difficulty, that of obtaining the consent of two-thirds of the Senate to the submission of such a proposal, but it also ignores the ominous circumstance that whereas the States have ratified twenty-one of the twenty-four or twenty-five Amendments thus far submitted to them, this small number comprised the sole survivors from the legislative gantlet of more than three thousand proposals. For all that, the suggestion may have merit, *provided* the Senate can be brought to realize that constitutional developments have so eaten away its prerogative that to continue to defend it is to court ultimate humiliation. The matter is of such importance that I make no apologies for going into it at some length.

The fact that the Constitutional Document has not been greatly altered by formal amendment so far as the make-up and powers of the National Government are concerned ought not be permitted to obscure the further fact that the *working* constitution to which the Document lends legal and moral sanction has from the first undergone constant changes. The stock illustration of the latter kind of constitutional change is furnished by the declension as early as 1796 of the "College of Electors," which is pictured in the *Federalist* as acting with almost superhuman aloofness from vulgar partisan prejudices and interests,[68] into a political sideshow of party marionettes. Another example is the emergence of the President's Cabinet, referred to a moment ago, and still another is the one we have just been considering, the rejection by the Senate at the outset of the role of collaborator with the President in the formulation of foreign policies for that of an independent organ vested with unrestricted power to criticize, amend, and reject such policies as reach it from the hands of the President in the shape of treaties. What, however, interests us in the present connection is the extent to which even this latter, negative role of the Senate has been affected by developments down the years. It is no exaggeration to say that a President who enjoys the support of reliable *legislative* majorities in the two houses is today in a constitutional position to elaborate his diplomatic policies with very little thought for the predilections of what the late John Hay baptized "the recalcitrant one-third plus one man of the Senate." Conversely *no* President, whatever support he is able to command in the Senate in getting its imprimatur affixed to his treaties, can pursue very long a foreign policy which lacks the legislative backing of *both* houses, for without this backing, or an outright *coup d'état*, taxes cannot be laid, funds paid out of the Treasury, the credit of the United States pledged, armies raised and supported, navies provided and maintained, or many other things done that the prosecution of a foreign policy is sure sooner or later to require.

We have already seen that the President's powers in the international field came early to approximate the prerogative of the British Crown; that Congress's powers in the same field are today the legislative powers of a centralized government; that both these vast reservoirs of "cognate powers" may be united in the hands of the President at the option of Congress.[69] Thus the doctrinal basis exists for a powerful direct assault upon "the recalcitrant one-third plus one man of the Senate." More than that, however, a wealth of precedents also exists which, even without the support lent them by the above principles of our Constitutional Law, would bode no good for the Senate's prerogative, and which with that support bodes considerably less. Such precedents fall into three main groups: (1) those which have rootage in the President's powers as organ of foreign relations and as Commander-in-Chief, whereof the "executive agreement" properly so-called is the outstanding illustration; (2) those which stem for the most part from Congress's enumerated powers, although they, too, frequently assume the shape of "executive agreements" in a looser sense of the term, in consequence of a delegation of power by Congress to the President;[70] (3) a group in which Congressional action takes on the characteristics of sovereign action.

1. An early instance of "treaty-making" by the President without the aid or consent of either Congress or the Senate was the exchange of notes in 1817 between the British Minister Bagot and Acting Secretary of State Rush for the limitation of naval forces on the Great Lakes. Not till a year afterward was it submitted to the Senate, by which it was promptly ratified. Nearly ninety years later occurred the parallel case, with appropriate deviations from the original model, of the first Roosevelt's treaty with Santo Domingo for putting the customs houses of that bankrupt nation under American control in order to forestall an attempt by its European creditors to seize them. When the Senate failed to ratify the treaty with reasonable promptitude the President proceeded to put it into force as an "executive agreement," whereupon the Senate, following one or two face-saving gestures, capitulated. And some years prior, in 1900, President McKinley had on his own sole authority as Commander-in-Chief, contributed a land force of 5,000 men and a naval force to cooperate with similar contingents from other Powers to rescue the legations in Peking from the Boxers; and a year later had, again without consulting either Congress or the Senate, accepted for the United States the Boxer Indemnity Protocol between China and the intervening Powers.

Outstanding among recent executive agreements is the Hull-Lothian agreement, whereby the President in the late summer of 1940, some sixteen months before we entered the war, handed over fifty units of the United States Navy to Great Britain in return for leases of certain sites for naval bases in the British West Indies and elsewhere. The transaction represented an invasion by the President of a field of power heretofore regarded as reserved by the Constitution (Article IV, section 3) to Congress exclusively, and overrode definite statutory provisions governing the disposal of over-age naval craft. Nevertheless, it was justified by the Attorney General as within the President's powers as Commander-in-Chief and as organ of foreign relations, and was to all intents and purposes ratified by Congress itself when it appropriated funds for the construction of the bases.[71]

A year later the President joined with the British Prime Minister in a formal declaration of "peace aims"—although the United States was not even yet in the war—which they christened "The Atlantic Charter."[72] While bearing some of the marks of a bilateral agreement between the two governments, the document is stamped by the vague generality of its terms rather as a proclamation to the world at large of the benevolent intentions of its eminent authors than as a state act intended to give rise to obligations in the technical sense.

From the Moscow Conference, on the other hand, issued several quite definite pledges to one another by the governments which were parties to it respecting future action, and the maturing of several of these is predicated for the period following the strictly military phase of the war. The recognition, however, in the fourth paragraph of the joint Four-Nation Declaration of "the necessity of establishing at the earliest practicable date a general international organization . . . for the maintenance of international peace and security," is again of the nature of a proclamation of intentions rather than, accurately speaking, an international act.[73]

Writers on the subject sometimes assume that "executive agreements" are sufficiently differentiated from "treaties," in the making of which the Senate participates, whenever the former can be explained as issuing from the President's prerogative as Commander-in-Chief or his power as organ of foreign relations. But obviously this mode of reasoning ignores the essential question, which is not whether the President can constitutionally enter into executive agreements with other governments—a point universally conceded—but what *scope* these may today validly take.

It is submitted that if an executive agreement is a convenient instrument for carrying out a conceded executive power —or if an executive agreement, in the broader sense of the term, is a convenient instrument for effectuating a power of Congress, or merged powers of President and Congress—then the employment of this method of reaching an understanding with another government cannot be warrantably characterized as an "evasion" of the treaty-making power in which the Senate participates. It is true that executive agreements of both sorts are resorted to nowadays much more freely than formerly, but ordinarily this is simply from the plain necessities of the case. Even the most convinced critic of the executive agreement device would scarcely contend that the President ought to go to the Senate every time he finds it desirable to arrive at a common understanding with one of our allies regarding matters of military policy. Yet if the President is not required by the Constitution to do this it is only because the subject-matter of the agreement, being within his power as Commander-in-Chief, was not removed therefrom by the circumstance that he was called upon, in order to exercise it most effectively, to covenant with the representatives of another government or other governments.

The truth seems to be that the critics of the executive agreement who raise the cry of "evasion" rest their case in the last analysis on the idea, never clearly expressed, that all constitutional development—by which they generally mean any departure from their own conception of what the Constitution means—ought to be by formal amendment, and that there is something essentially dishonest about constitutional changes which are brought about by practice and usage, at least as soon as such changes have reached the stage where people become generally conscious of them. I should be disposed to contend, to the very contrary, that *the most beneficial type of constitutional change is that which issues gradually from, and so has been thoroughly tested by, successful practice.* To be sure, there are often limits to the possibilities of this type of constitutional change under a written constitution like our own, and there are occasions when the amending process ought to be resorted to in order to round out and perfect some change which long practice has shown to be desirable.

From another angle it has been argued at times that executive agreements, in contradistinction to treaties, are not, unless they were initially authorized or have been subsequently approved by Congress, "law of the land," and hence are not noticeable by the courts. But if this was ever sound doctrine, it is no longer so in view of the explicit holding of the Court in 1937 in *United States v. Belmont*,[74] which was one of the Russian Insurance Cases referred to earlier. The point at issue in the Belmont Case was whether a district court of the United States was free to dismiss an action by the United States, as assignee of the Soviet government, for certain moneys which were once the property of a Russian corporation whose assets had been appropriated by the Soviet government. The Court, speaking by Justice Sutherland, held not. The President's act in recognizing the Soviet government, and the accompanying agreements, constituted, said the Justice, an international compact which the President, "as the sole organ" of international relations for the United States, was authorized to enter upon without consulting the Senate. Nor did State laws and policies make any difference in such a situation; for while the supremacy of treaties is established by the Constitution in express terms, yet the same rule holds "in the case of all international compacts and agreements from the very fact that complete power over international affairs is in the National Government and is not and cannot be subject to any curtailment or interference on the part of the several States."[75]

*Not only, therefore, may executive agreements have the force of law—they may have the force of "supreme law of the land."* What is more, if the "Fifty Destroyer Deal"—the Hull-Lothian agreement—is to be considered as illustrating the law and the doctrine in such matters, an executive agreement is capable also of overriding prior acts of Congress. To be sure, a treaty is in theory capable of doing this too (see section on Constitutional *v.* International Obligation, on page 28), although I venture to question if the cases, when closely examined, really bear out the theory. But that the "Fifty Destroyer Deal" repealed certain Congressional legislation for the purposes of that particular transaction is clear and undeniable.[76]

Nor can it be admitted on the basis either of principle or

of precedent that, as some have contended, the international obligation of the United States under an executive agreement resting on Presidential power alone terminates with the Administration which entered into it. Conceding that the agreement was within the power of the President, that is to say, of the constitutionally recognized organ of foreign relations, to make in the first place, the nation is bound by it according to its plain terms and intent just as truly as it would be by a treaty. At least, if this is not so, I should like to know just why it is not. To be sure, many if not the majority of executive agreements merely mark the completion of a transaction, are "executed" on the spot, as it were, while still others, although "executory" in nature, are *ad interim* arrangements which are intended to be replaced ultimately by some more formal one. Nevertheless, it took the Washington Conference and at least two solemn treaties to rid us of the incubus of the Lansing-Ishii agreement of 1917; while the "gentlemen's agreement," first drawn in 1907, by which Japanese immigration to this country was regulated for some seventeen years, was finally put an end to only by an act of Congress. Furthermore, the actual effect of an executive agreement on the foreign policy of the country, and thereby on its future welfare, may be quite as extensive as if the agreement had been a full panoplied treaty. Thus the "Fifty Destroyer Deal," although its immediate and inducing purpose will have been accomplished with the end of the present war, creates nonetheless a relationship between the United States and Great Britain of the nature of a regional defensive alliance, one which will survive the war.

2. We turn now to those precedents which stem primarily from Congress's enumerated powers. Some of these, as was noted above, spring immediately from a delegation of power by Congress to the President and so take the form of "executive agreements" in the broader sense of the term, the outstanding illustrations being the so-called "foreign trade pacts," of which Secretary Hull is today so effective an exponent. The McKinley Tariff Act of 1890 furnished an ambiguous

authorization for the earliest of these, the constitutionality of which was attacked on the ground both that they represented a delegation of legislative power to the President and that they invaded the field of jurisdiction of the treaty-making power; but in the leading case of *Field v. Clark*[77] both contentions were overruled, the latter without further comment by the Court than its general observation that the challenged provision was a "necessary and proper" law for carrying Congress's power to regulate foreign commerce into effect. The precedent and supporting doctrine thus established have since been gradually expanded until by the Act of 1934, which was renewed in 1937, 1940, and again in 1943, the President is authorized to lower customs rates as much as fifty per cent on imports from other countries in order to obtain equivalent concessions from them. Nor is the validity of the agreements by which such legislation is implemented longer open to serious question in view of the decisions.

Yet that the same results could be obtained by treaty is certain. Indeed, in 1787 and for long afterward, that is the very way in which comparable results were obtained. So what this line of precedents establishes is that *if the subject-matter to be regulated falls within the powers of Congress, the latter may constitutionally authorize the President to deal with it by negotiation and agreement with other governments, the treaty-making power to the contrary notwithstanding.*

A further illustration of the same principle is afforded by the Act of February 9, 1922, by which a commission was created to effect agreements covering the debts owed this country by certain other governments. Since these agreements were to be laid before Congress, not before the Senate in its treaty-making capacity, Senator Walsh of Montana protested the measure as unconstitutional, a contention which Senator McCumber of North Dakota answered with the sweeping assertion that "anything done by treaty could be done by statute."[78] And unquestionably what was done by statute on this occasion, by warrant presumably of Congress's power to dispose of property of the United States, could have been done by treaty by virtue of the fact that the subject was one the settlement of which unavoidably involved international negotiation and agreement.

Similarly the Lend-Lease Act of March 11, 1941, is the fountainhead of the numerous Mutual Aid agreements under which our government has to date furnished our allies in the present war some fifteen billions worth of munitions of war and other supplies. In the case, on the other hand, of the United Nations Relief and Rehabilitation Convention which was drawn by a conference of United Nations representatives at Hot Springs, Virginia, last June, a different course has been adopted, but one which seems likely to lead to the same general result. It was originally the intention of the State Department to treat the convention as an executive agreement, but protests from certain Senators against this procedure led to a series of conferences between representatives of the Department and a subcommittee of the Foreign Relations Committee which led to a revision of the convention in certain particulars and a pledge by the subcommittee to recommend its validation by an act of Congress authorizing appropriations to carry it out, and apparently this plan is being followed. It is interesting to note that Senator Vandenberg, who was one of the Senate subcommittee and approved the compromise plan just mentioned, took the position earlier that the convention was in every respect a treaty.[79]

So, where the path of Congressional power and that of the treaty-making power have crossed, it is the former which has usually held the walk. One further illustration, a relatively early one, will not be out of place. For five years, from 1866 to 1871, Congress, which has power to "regulate commerce with the Indian tribes," refused to enact legislation to carry Indian treaties into effect, and in the latter year passed an act which peremptorily "denied the right of any Indian tribe or nation to be recognized as an independent nation for treaty-making purposes," thereby transferring all Indian affairs to its jurisdiction; and this was done in face of the fact that among the first fruits of the treaty-making power were certain treaties with Indian tribes.[80] Nevertheless, the decision of the Supreme Court in 1886 in *United States v. Kagama*[81] underwrites this outright appropriation by Congress of unlimited authority over a subject-matter as to which its prior authority had been definitely limited.

3. But the most striking cases of the treaty-making process being superseded by the legislative are those which have occurred in direct consequence of the breakdown of the former, either actual or prospective. Thus it was by simple Congressional resolution that Texas was annexed in 1845 after the Upper Chamber had defeated a treaty for the same purpose. It was thus that Hawaii was annexed in 1898 after a treaty for the purpose had been blocked by a group of Cleveland Democrats; and it is altogether probable that the Philippines would have been acquired in the same manner the following year had the Senate eliminated, as it seemed likely for a time to do, the applicable provision of the Treaty of Paris. Likewise, it was by a joint resolution that war with the Central Powers was finally terminated July 2, 1921, following the defeat of the Treaty of Versailles.[82] Also, it was by a joint resolution, passed June 19, 1934, that Congress authorized the President to accede to Part XIII of the Treaty of Versailles, establishing the International Labor Office.[83]

But now it should be observed as to this third group of precedents that, except possibly the one first mentioned, in support of which the historically unallowable argument was concocted at the time that Congress was merely exercising its power to admit "new States into this Union," *all of them exemplify Congress's indefinite power in the field of foreign relations, its power, in other words, as the legislative organ of a nation which is sovereign at International Law. But while they exemplify this power, they do not demarcate its scope or extent. This, in principle, must be as great as the external requirements of the nation itself, provided only that the power does not in its exercise run counter to some specific limitation of the Constitution; and the prerogative of the*

*Senate in the making of treaties does not, as the precedents which have just been reviewed attest, comprise such a limitation.* Suppose then that the dominant sentiment of the country should find itself frustrated by a "recalcitrant one-third plus one man of the Senate" in its efforts to put our government into an international organization for the maintenance of peace, would the country have to reconcile itself to such an obvious breakdown of constitutional machinery? I see no reason why it should do so any more than it did do so on the occasions just reviewed; and I see several reasons why it should not.

The Senate, being composed of two members from each State regardless of size of population, is peculiarly unfitted by the very principle of its make-up to be the custodian of a power requiring an extraordinary majority for its exercise. Nor does the argument in support of this assertion necessarily involve an appeal to the supposed theoretical requirements of *democracy*—if I may anticipate a possible objection. The criticism which Hamilton, certainly no democrat, levels in *Federalist 22* against the Articles of Confederation in their entirety applies almost to the dotting of its "i's" and the crossing of its "t's" to the participation of the Senate in the treaty-making function, and always has. Let me quote Hamilton's words: "The right of equal suffrage among the States is another exceptionable part of the Confederation. Every idea of proportion and every rule of fair representation conspire to condemn a principle, which gives to Rhode Island an equal weight in the scale of power with Massachusetts, or Connecticut, or New York; and to Delaware an equal voice in the national deliberations with Pennsylvania, or Virginia, or North Carolina. Its operation contradicts the fundamental maxim of republican government, which requires that the sense of the majority should prevail."

But, it may be contended, Hamilton goes on to recite, that the departure which the principle of "equal suffrage among the States" marks from the principle of majority rule is harmless because all important decisions of the Confederation have

[ 47 ]

to be made by a vote of nine states, "and it may be thence inferred, that nine States would always comprehend a majority of the Union." This argument he counters as follows: "What at first sight may seem a remedy, is, in reality, a poison. To give a minority a negative upon the majority (which is always the case where more than a majority is requisite to a decision), is, in its tendency, to subject the sense of the greater number to that of the lesser. . . . The necessity of unanimity in public bodies, or of something approaching towards it, has been founded upon a supposition that it would contribute to security. But its real operation is to embarrass the administration, to destroy the energy of the government, and to substitute the pleasure, caprice, or artifices of an insignificant, turbulent, or corrupt junto, to the regular deliberations and decisions of a respectable majority. . . . The public business must, in some way or other, go forward. If a pertinacious minority can control the opinion of a majority, respecting the best mode of conducting it, the majority, in order that something may be done, must conform to the views of the minority; and thus the sense of the smaller number will overrule that of the greater, and give a tone to the national proceedings. Hence, tedious delays; continual negotiation and intrigue; contemptible compromises of the public good. . . . When the concurrence of a large number is required by the Constitution to the doing of any national act, we are apt to rest satisfied that all is safe, because nothing improper will be likely *to be done*; but we forget how much good may be prevented, and how much ill may be produced, by the power of hindering the doing what may be necessary, and of keeping affairs in the same unfavorable posture in which they may happen to stand at particular periods."

In short, to apply Hamilton's argument to the present issue, *the anomaly presented by the two-thirds rule is vastly aggravated by the principle of equal representation of the States in the Senate*; and if this was true in 1788, it is doubly, trebly true today. Thus, whereas in 1788 a "recalcitrant one-third plus one man of the Senate" could not have been recruited from States containing less than one-seventh of the population, an equally lethal combination can today be compounded out of Senators representing less than one-thirteenth thereof. And that the staid-moving world of 1788 produced many fewer situations requiring positive action, and prompt action, by government than does our own "split-second world," is too obvious a consideration to require more than mention. To be sure, nobody is proposing that we get rid of equal representation of the States in the Senate—that apparently is with us to stay. But this fact of itself becomes on the above showing another argument in favor of the legislative route into international commitments.

But in fact we of today are not free, as Hamilton was, to ignore the theoretical demands of democracy, we who stand at the receiving end, as it were, of that whole course of development whereby the National Government and its procedures have been progressively democratized from the beginning. I must say, therefore, that I find very persuasive the views recently expressed by the author of the Fulbright Resolution regarding the relative validity of Senate and Congressional approval of treaties. I quote again:

"I submit [says Mr. Fulbright] that an undertaking approved by a majority of the House of Representatives and of the Senate is just as solemn as action by two-thirds of the Senate. . . , such action by both houses is more binding, has greater validity, greater permanency and consistency for the future than has a policy imposed by the power of obstruction, possessed by thirty-four [sic] Senators who, in any given instance, probably will represent a very small fraction of our total population. It seems to me that to be consistent and positive over the years our foreign policy must be supported by the majority of our people. I do not think that one can deny that the House of Representatives is, on the whole, more responsive to, and more truly reflective of, the will of the people than any other body in our government. The fact that they must be elected every two years by relatively small constituencies induces in them a genuine humility and a profound respect for the will of the people. It prevents the growth of that detached arrogance which sometimes accompanies a long and secure tenure of power.

"If this is true of the Representatives, then it seems to me that . . . the most 'binding sanction' would be that procedure which more accurately than any other translates into definite action the will of the greatest number of our citizens. This procedure is, I submit, a joint resolution approved by not less than a majority of both houses of the Congress."[84]

And let me in emphasis of Mr. Fulbright's words repeat something I said earlier: The Senate's imprimatur, however unanimously or enthusiastically given, is not going to guarantee that the United States will continue a helpful member of an international organization. That can be assured, so far as the government can assure it, only by the President and Congress, the national Executive power and the national Legislative power. Once the Senate has acted in its treaty-making capacity it is *functus officio*—a god remote, unconcerned for the results of its single generative act.

Finally, this point is perhaps worth considering even though not strictly relevant to the immediate purpose of this inquiry. The anxious question, What will the Senate do? is prompted by what happened to the League of Nations Covenant twenty-five years ago, and that may turn out to have very little bearing on the way in which peace will come about after the present war. Only very recently General Smuts, observing that after the war America, Britain, and Russia would hold world power, made the prediction that peace "would come very slowly, perhaps so slowly as never to make possible a peace conference at all, but only a comprehensive armistice that would permit a long process of working out solutions."[85] Are such solutions to be referred when and as they occur for the approval of the Senate? As a matter of fact, they are at this moment in course of being worked out without any account being taken of the Senate, and not merely at Cairo and Teheran, but in less conspicuous theaters of action. Only a few days after General Smuts's outgiving and as if to point it up, Secretary of the Navy Knox informed the country, *via* the English Speaking Union of Chicago, that the existing collaboration at sea of the American and British navies would be continued after the war as a "peace patrol."[86] Yet nobody has risen to question the competence of the President to enter into such an arrangement. The matter need not be elaborated; what it boils down to is this: that the final instrument for setting up an international organization for the maintenance of peace is likely to embody already established institutions and practices from which the United States could not withdraw without serious loss both moral and material. And the durability of such arrangements is going to depend far more upon favoring action by the President and favoring legislation by Congress than on a vote of consent of the Senate which, from the necessities of the case, must be largely perfunctory.

One of the authors of that much parented but abortive prodigy of statesmanship, the "$B_2H_2$ Resolution" (S.R. 114), is quoted as saying: "The whole world knows and our Allies know that it is this United States Senate which will finally decide what will be the foreign policy of our country when the war ends."[87] When confronted with the resolution itself and its unimpressive outcome, this very confident pronouncement sounds somewhat bombastic. The resolution urged American leadership (step A), "in calling meetings of representatives of the United Nations" (step B), "for the purpose of forming an organization of the United Nations" (step C), "with specific and limited authority" to do five different things (steps D, E, F, G, and H).[88] Although the resolution never even came to a vote in the Foreign Relations Committee, let alone in the Senate, three of the five things it listed had either been done already, or have since been done by the United Nations without benefit of the advice and consent of the Senate.

The Connally Resolution (S.R. 172), which was passed by the Senate on November 5, by the overwhelming vote of 85 to 5, is a rather different affair. After declaring in favor of waging the war "until complete victory is achieved," the resolution further resolves:

"That the United States cooperate with its comrades-in-arms in securing a just and honorable peace.

"That the United States, acting through its constitutional processes, join with free and sovereign nations in the establishment and maintenance of international authority with power to prevent aggression and to preserve the peace of the world.

"That the Senate recognizes the necessity of there being established at the earliest practicable date a general international organization, based on the principle of the sovereign equality of all peace-loving States, and open to membership by all such States, large and small, for the maintenance of international peace and security.

"That, pursuant to the Constitution of the United States, any treaty made to effect the purposes of this resolution, on behalf of the Government of the United States with any other nation or any association of nations, shall be made only by and with the advice and consent of the Senate of the United States, provided two-thirds of the Senators present concur."[89]

The first thing to be noted about this phraseology is its complete lack of dogmatic assertion regarding the Senate's treaty prerogative. Not only is the term "constitutional processes" (in the second paragraph) noncommittal, but so too is the statement as to treaty-making in the fourth paragraph, which says, in effect, that *if* the United States elects to enter an international organization by the treaty route, the treaty will have to be approved by the Senate, by a two-thirds vote of the Senators present, a statement which nobody who has read the Constitution will be apt to question. For the rest, the resolution is a pledge of good behavior on the Senate's part if it is consulted in its treaty-making capacity—a pledge which is couched in almost the identical terms of the fourth article of the Moscow Declaration. Nor is this absence of last-ditch truculence from the resolution at all difficult to account for. The Senate is increasingly aware that, caught between the juridical situation which has been sketched in the preceding pages, on the one hand, and the rising sentiment of the country in favor of American participation in an international organization for the maintenance of peace on the other hand, its position is today not unlike that of the Supreme Court following the 1936 elections, and it wisely proposes to endeavor to put its house in order betimes. The resolution is at once an assurance to the American public and a warning to all potential or budding "recalcitrant one-third plus one man" combinations among the Senate's own membership. There is every reason, therefore, for answering the question under discussion in this Section in the negative.

To sum up: The Senate's role in the conduct of American foreign relations has been from the start a diminishing role. First, it was to be sole legatee of the Congress of the Confederation in this respect; then it was to collaborate as a council with the President throughout the entire process of treaty-making; finally, as early as the Jay Treaty, it found itself reduced to the role of critic and censor of Presidential projects, although with a quasi-legislative power to amend them. In this last capacity, to be sure, the two-thirds rule afforded the Senate great strength, yet an unmerited strength, in that the rule was based in part at least on the early discredited assumption of conciliar collaboration, while today it is completely out of line with the democratic assumptions which have generally come to underlie the functioning Constitution, and all the more so because of the principle on which it is constructed. And in other ways too the Senate's prerogative has become an anachronism. The sectional jealousies which accounted to some extent for the Senate being given this prerogative in 1787 have long since disappeared, and if others have taken their place they are subordinate to the predominant interest of the country as a whole, whereof Congress in its legislative capacity is a far better representative than the Senate alone. Furthermore, the dependence in the long run of any President for Congress's legislative support of his foreign policies, something which the Convention of 1787 apparently overlooked completely, renders the Senate's treaty role a fifth wheel to the governmental coach, and a fifth wheel of a very cumbrous and out-of-date model when we consider the Senate's characteristic methods of transacting business. But most of all is the anomalous character of the Senate's prerogative attested by the devices to which the practical conduct of our foreign relations has first and last given rise for its avoidance. When taken in conjunction with certain doctrines of American Constitutional Law, and especially the doctrine that Congress's legislative power in the field of foreign relations is that of the nation itself, *these devices provide the United States an alternative route into an international organization for the maintenance of peace, one which from the point of view of the requirements both of democracy and of sound government is the preferable route.*

So why should not the Senate recognize these facts, and recognizing them take appropriate action? In other words, *why should it not at once put itself back of a proposal to replace the existing provision in the Constitution for Senate approval of treaties by one requiring legislative approval?* For thus would it do its part toward removing by one and the same stroke whatever possibilities for mischief still remain from an outmoded constitutional procedure and the equal possibilities for humiliation to itself if that procedure should ever be made the instrument for blocking the clear demands of American public opinion.

# EPILOGUE

WITH the possible exception of the Civil War, the impact of World War II upon our institutions is the most massive force to which they have ever been subjected, and the shape which they will assume after they finally emerge from that unparalleled pressure is still to be determined. One thing, nevertheless, can be said at once. The chief beneficiary of the current war effort will be, in terms of governing power, the Presidency, as ultimately it has been of every great war in which this country has taken part in the past.

We have thus shared in some measure, and are destined to share further, in a movement which has elsewhere attained the dimensions of disaster, and the results of which we are today combatting on a dozen fronts scattered over the globe. Throughout the greater part of the nineteenth century the strong flow of power was from the executive to the legislative. That is what the spread of political liberalism signified. So far this century this flow has been sharply reversed and before the resurging current constitutional governments have toppled even in some countries where they had long seemed part of a solidly established order.

What was the cause of this reactionary movement, so disappointing to the prophecies of less than a generation ago, when the world was being made safe for democracy, so calamitous to human freedom? First and last, the most efficient cause was war actual or threatened, and the necessity which states have been under not only of conducting their foreign relations, but also of planning their domestic economies, in the shadow of this constant menace, which has progressively deepened as war has become more terrible.

So today the maintenance of constitutional government in the United States becomes linked with the broader cause of its restoration and preservation elsewhere. This broader cause is, however, one which we can aid in the long run only collaterally, through the foreign policies we choose to pursue. Time was when our dominant position in the Western Hemisphere and the Monroe Doctrine, which vocalized this dominance, assured us against becoming involved in extracontinental wars, and thereby protected free institutions among us. Unfortunately that assurance no longer holds, a fact of which our entry into two world wars within a generation is certainly sufficient proof.

What choices, then, are left us in the realm of foreign policy? I see only two: *imperialistic adventuring* and *the active promotion of world peace*, and which of these alternatives is likely to supply the more favorable conditions for the continuance of constitutional democracy among us is hardly open to reasonable doubt. Yet even wars fought for the most generous ends can still spell disaster for that complex set of values which our Constitution aims to uphold and promote. In World War I we sought no territorial or other gains for ourselves except some guarantee that the peace following it would be a lasting one. Nevertheless, it was following this war that so sober and conservative a thinker as former Chief Justice Hughes raised the question whether, "in view of the precedents now established . . . constitutional government as heretofore maintained in this Republic would survive another great war even victoriously waged."[90]

That question is still unanswered and, as I implied above, will probably remain unanswered for some time to come. But the question itself bears witness to the fact that the *cause of peace abroad and the cause of constitutional democracy at home are allied causes*, and must be so treated by those whose lot it will be to forge our foreign policies in the years to come.

And as this study shows, there are no substantial constitutional obstacles to the pursuit by our government of a foreign policy which has as its main objective the maintenance of international peace, while as to Sovereignty I repeat: *When Total War is the price of Total Sovereignty, the price is too high*. What, indeed, is "Sovereignty," as we see it daily at work, except the freedom of decision and action with which the Constitution and laws endow our governing agencies; and always the important question is: How can this freedom of decision and action be exercised by such agencies so as to serve best the real freedom of the American People, their "unalienable right" to "life, liberty and the pursuit of happiness"?

# NOTES

1. Josef L. Kunz, "The 'Vienna School' and International Law," *New York Univ. L. Q. R.*, XI, 1-52 (1934); same, "La Primauté du Droit de Gens," *Revue de Droit International et de Legislation Comparée*, 3rd series, VI, 556-98 (1925).

2. J. B. Moore, *International Law Digest*, I, 1-9.

3. C. G. Fenwick, *International Law* (1924), 276-7.

4. W. W. Willoughby, *The Fundamental Concepts of Public Law*, 282-308; Albert Kocourek, "The Century of Jurisprudence since John Austin," *Law, A Century of Progress*, II, 195-230 (1937); Harold Laski, *The Foundations of Sovereignty* (1921), 17.

5. *The Cherokee Tobacco*, 11 Wall. 616 (1871).

6. 14 Pet. 540, 575-6.

7. 3 Dall. 199.

8. *Ibid.*, 236-7.

9. The present writer's *National Supremacy*, 59-98.

10. 11 Pet. 102.

11. *Ibid.*, 139.

12. *Prevost v. Greneaux*, 19 How. 1, at 7.

13. *Frederickson v. La.*, 23 How. 445, at 448.

14. 100 U.S. 483.

15. 7 Cr. 603 (1813).

16. 252 U.S. 416.

17. 289 U.S. 48.

18. *Ibid.*, 59.

19. 312 U.S. 100.

20. No. 23.

21. Address before the Am. Bar Assoc., Sept. 5, 1917. Sixteen years later, however, Chief Justice Hughes speaks of "The War Power" in the singular, and describes it as follows: "It is the power to wage war successfully and thus it permits the harnessing of the entire energies of the people in a supreme cooperative effort to preserve the nation." *Home Building and Loan Assoc. v. Blaisdell*, 290 U.S. 398, at 426 (1934).

22. 3 Dall. 54.

23. *Ibid.*, 74.

24. 12 Wall. 457, at 554-6.

25. 130 U.S. 581.

26. *Ibid.*, 604.

27. *Fong Yue Ting v. U.S.*, 149 U.S. 698, at 711.

28. 299 U.S. 304.

29. *Ibid.*, 317-8.

30. *Op. cit.*, in note 9, at 121-4.

31. *Esprit des Lois*, Bk. XI, ch. 6.

32. *Willoughby on the Constitution* (2nd Ed.), III, 1616-20; Malcolm Sharp, "The Classical American Doctrine of the Separation of Powers," *Selected Essays on Constitutional Law*, IV, 168-94 (1938); also Madison in *Federalist* 47.

33. See Section II. D, on page 28.

34. 2 Pet. 253.

35. *Ibid.*, 308.

36. See the present writer's *The President's Control of Foreign Relations*, 163-7.

37. On the sources and growth of the concept of "executive power" under the Constitution, see my *The President, Office and Powers*, 1-30 *passim*, 64, 78-80, 82-3, 86, 92-4, 95, 97-9, 111, 112-7 *passim*, 123, 126-36 *passim*, 210-2, 228, 241, 247, 374, 396.

38. *Op. cit.*, in note 36, at 16-30.

39. *Op. cit.*, in note 37, at 403-4.

40. Ch. XI, §141 (Morley, ed.).

41. See e.g. 307 U.S. 588, 603-8.

42. Note 28.

43. Art. I, sec. 9, and "The Bill of Rights."

44. *Op. cit.*, in note 9, ch. II; *op. cit.*, note 37, at 164-6, 192, 393-4. But, of course, private rights even of citizens are subject in time of war to restraints that would be unallowable in time of peace. In the words of Justice Sutherland in *United States v. Macintosh*, decided in 1931: "To the end that war may not result in defeat, freedom of speech may, by act of Congress, be curtailed or denied so that the morale of the people and the spirit of the army may not be broken by seditious utterances; freedom of the press curtailed to preserve our military plans and movements from the knowledge of the enemy; deserters and spies put to death without indictment or trial by jury; ships and supplies requisitioned; property of alien enemies, theretofore under the protection of the Constitution, seized without process and converted to the public use without compensation and without due process of law in the ordinary sense of that term; prices of food and other necessities of life fixed or regulated; railways taken over and operated by the government; and other drastic powers, wholly inadmissible in time of peace, exercised, to meet the emergencies of war." 283 U.S. 605, at 622.

45. Note 7.

46. 3 Dall. at 245. See also *Lattimer v. Poteet*, 14 Pet. 4, at 14 (1840).

47. 315 U.S. 203.

48. *Ibid.*, 252-3.

49. S. B. Crandall, *Treaties, Their Making and Enforcement* (2nd Ed.), 170-1.

50. See *op. cit.*, in note 32, at I, 549-50.

51. 5 *Opinions*, 333, 345; 6 *ibid.*, 291; 13 *ibid.*, 354.

52. 112 U.S. 580.

53. Note 25.

54. 130 U.S. at 600. The reader should recall that the power which Congress exercised in repealing the treaty with China was its *inherent, sovereign* power to exclude aliens from American territory. See p. 18 above.

55. 112 U.S. at 598. See also note 5 above.

56. Art. IX.

57. Farrand, *Records*, II, 183.

58. *Ibid.*, 392-4, 498-9, 538, 540-1.

59. In *Federalist* 64, written by Jay, the relation of the Senate to the President in the business of treaty-making is depicted throughout as that of a council.

Speaking in the Senate in 1818, Rufus King said: "In these concerns the Senate are the Constitutional and the only responsible counsellors of the President. And in this capacity the Senate may, and ought to, look into and watch over every branch of the foreign affairs of the nation; they may, therefore, at any time call for full and exact information respecting the foreign affairs, and express their opinion and advice to the President respecting the same, when, and under whatever other circumstances, they may think such advice expedient.

"There is a peculiar jealousy manifested in the Constitution concerning the power which shall manage the foreign affairs, and make treaties with foreign nations. Hence the provision which requires the consent of two-thirds of the Senators to confirm any compact with a foreign nation that shall bind the United States; thus putting it in the power of a minority of the Senators, or States to control the President and a majority of the Senate: a check on the Executive power to be found in no other case.

"To make a treaty includes all the proceedings by which it is made; and the advice and consent of the Senate being necessary in the making of treaties, must necessarily be so, touching the measures employed in making the same. The Constitution does not say that treaties shall be concluded, but that they shall be made, by and with the advice and consent of the Senate; none therefore can be made without such advice and consent; and the objections against the agency of the Senate in making treaties, or in advising the President to make the same, cannot be sustained, but by giving to the Constitution an interpretation different from its obvious and most salutary meaning." *Farrand*, III, 424-5; *cf. ibid.*, 269.

King had been a member of the Philadelphia Convention. The interest of the South and Southwest in obtaining the right to navigate the lower Mississippi, which the East was quite ready to sacrifice, was the sectional interest closest to the hearts of several members of the Convention. *Ibid.*, 306-7.

60. *Op. cit.*, in note 37, at 232.

61. Ralston Hayden, *The Senate and Treaties*, 149-53.

62. *Op. cit.*, in note 37, at 80-1.

63. *Op. cit.*, in note 61, ch. VIII.

64. S.R. 114 (78th Cong., 1st sess.); *N.Y. Times*, Mar. 14, 1943.

65. *Ibid.*, Sept. 25, 1943.

66. *Constitutional Government in the United States*, 138 and 141. For an excellent critical account of the evolution of the Senate's role in treaty-making, see Lindsay Rogers, *The American Senate*, 54-87.

67. *N.Y. Times*, Aug. 29, 1943.

68. No. 68.

69. Chap. II, §§ A, 3 and B, at pages 17-20 and 22-24.

70. Much of the illustrative data in the following paragraphs of the text is from my *President, Office and Powers*, 236-8 and 413-5. For a wealth of similar material see Wallace McClure's *International Executive Agreements, Democratic Procedure under the Constitution of the United States* (1941). About nine hundred treaties were proclaimed by Presidents between 1789 and 1929, while another two hundred plus never became effective on account of adverse action—or inaction—of the Senate. In the same period over 1,200 agreements were consummated with foreign countries, without the consent of the Senate. Kenneth Colegrove, *The American Senate and World Peace* (1944), 96. The State Department inaugurated the separate *Executive Agreement Series*, Oct. 1929. In the decade following more than one hundred executive agreements were made simply by an exchange of notes between our own and the other contracting government or governments. David M. Levitan, 35 *Ill. L.R.*, 365 (December, 1940).

71. *N.Y. Times*, Sept. 4, 1940; McClure, *op. cit.*, 394-403.

72. *Ibid.*, Aug. 25, 1941. On January 1, 1942, the Charter was embodied in the Declaration of the United Nations, subscribed to by twenty-six powers. *Ibid.*, Jan. 2, 1942. The Declaration, however, contains one binding pledge, a promise by the parties to it not to conclude a separate peace with any of the enemy powers.

73. *Ibid.*, Nov. 2, 1943. The following matter from an editorial in the *Times* of Nov. 3, 1943, provides a good summary of the Moscow agreements, as well as an instructive effort to square them with the editorial writer's conception of the line that should be drawn between the power of the President in the making of agreements and the treaty-making power in which the Senate participates:

"The first promise made at Moscow in the name of the United States is that this country will regard Hitler's annexation of Austria in 1938 as 'null and void' and will work for the liberation of that state from German domination. There can be no possible doubt that this is properly a question for Executive, and not for Senatorial, decision. This is quite in line with President Hoover's action in holding Japan's annexation of Manchuria to be null and void—and no voice in the Senate has ever been lifted to dispute the authority of this decision.

"The second promise made at Moscow is that the United States, at the time of the granting of any armistice to Germany, will demand the surrender of war criminals for punishment. It is the President, and not Congress, who must decide, in cooperation with our allies, what the terms of any armistice will be, and the inclusion of a demand for the surrender of war criminals is as properly a part of an armistice as a demand for the surrender of planes and cannon.

"The third promise at Moscow is that the United States, pending the ultimate free choice of the Italian people regarding their own future form of government, will use the authority of its arms in Italy to destroy the grip of the Fascist party and to promote the establishment of democratic institutions. As Commander in Chief of our armed forces engaged in the military occupation of any foreign territory, it is within the President's authority, and it is in fact his duty, to determine, with our allies, how our military occupation will be conducted.

"The fourth promise made at Moscow (Point 2 in the Four-Power Declaration) is a promise not to seek a separate peace: the President engages us to 'act together [with our allies] in all matters relating to the surrender and disarmament of the enemy.' It is his duty, and not the duty of the Senate, to decide with the armed forces when an armistice will be concluded. It is his prerogative to decide when he will submit a treaty to the Senate.

"The fifth promise made at Moscow (Point 3 in the Four-Power Declaration) grows out of the preceding one. It is a promise to cooperate with our allies in taking all measures 'deemed to be necessary to provide against any violation of the terms [of the armistice] imposed upon the enemy.' This is essentially a military question.

"The sixth and seventh promises made at Moscow (Points 5 and 6 in the Four-Power Declaration) look beyond the armistice terms to the interregnum between the end of the actual fighting and the conclusion of a formal peace. Here the President makes two pledges. He pledges us to consult with our allies 'as occasion requires . . . with a view to joint action on behalf of the community of nations.' And he pledges us, as our allies pledge themselves, not to employ our military forces 'within the territory of other states' except for the broad purpose of maintaining order. These are properly administrative questions. They are not questions for the Senate. The Senate is not an executive agency. It will be no more in a position to decide how our troops can best be used to maintain order, when the fighting ends, than it is now in position to decide when and where and how our troops can best be ordered into battle. . . .

"With the eighth promise made at Moscow (Point 4 in the Four-Power Declaration) we come to the longer future and the problem of organizing peace on a permanent basis. Necessarily this will involve a treaty, or several treaties, and here for the first time the Senate's authority properly comes into play. But note this: the President does not attempt to 'by-pass' the Senate and commit the United States, at this time and on his own authority, to membership in an organization to maintain international peace. He merely commits the United States—and the language here is very explicit—to *recognize the necessity of establishing at the earliest practicable date* an organization of this kind. It is for the Senate to confirm our membership. The Senate's prerogatives are carefully observed. And the form of organization favored by the President is precisely that favored in the post-war resolution now before the Senate: 'a general organization, based on the principles of the sovereign equality of all peace-loving states, and open to membership by all such states, large and small, for the maintenance of international peace and security.' This might almost be a paraphrase of the Connally resolution.

"The ninth and last promise made at Moscow (Point 7 in the Four-Power Declaration) is a pledge to 'confer and cooperate' with other United Nations 'to bring about a practicable general agreement with respect to the regulation of armaments in the post-war period.' This is only a pledge to see what can be done some day. The Senate's power to approve or to veto any ultimate agreement is in no way jeopardized.

"The case is clear that the Moscow agreements are thoroughly within the framework of the American constitutional system, with the President properly

[ 63 ]

exercising his power of initiative in the field of foreign affairs and the Senate's authority in the field of treaty-ratification properly respected."

One or two comments are in point. The editorial writer's statement that "the eighth promise made at Moscow" "might be a paraphrase of the Connally resolution" reverses the order of events. The probability is that both the "eighth promise" and this clause of the Connally Resolution came from a common source—the Department of State. The argument that the sixth and seventh promises deal with "administrative matters" and hence presented no questions proper for the Senate to consider, seems to me particularly weak as regards the sixth promise, which certainly implies that conclusions arrived at as the result of consultation will be followed by "joint action on behalf of the community of nations" fairly promptly.

It should be noted too that the editorial writer endeavors to fit "the first promise" into his scheme merely by a reference to precedent, which, to say the least, evades the issue.

74. 301 U.S. 324.

75. *Ibid.*, 330-2. In his recent volume *The Republic*, at page 217, Professor Beard quite justifiably takes Justice Sutherland to task for the rather extravagant language the latter uses at one point to describe the President's role as organ of foreign relations, but the criticism is itself open to criticism as being based on the silences of the Constitutional Document without sufficient account being taken of the verdict of actual practice under the Document.

76. See the present writer in the *New York Times* of Oct. 13, 1940.

77. 143 U.S. 649 (1892); also *Hampton v. U.S.*, 276 U.S. 394 (1928).

78. *Op. cit.*, in note 37, at 413.

79. *N.Y. Times*, July 9, Aug. 18, and 19, 1943, and Jan. 13, Feb. 18, 1944; also Kenneth Colegrove, *op. cit.*, 28-31 and 92-5. Legislation to authorize the transfer of certain lands in Panama to the Panama government and to carry out other provisions of an agreement negotiated by the Department of State was attacked in the Senate Dec. 3, 1942, as an effort to "by-pass the Senate," but was passed by the Senate the following day. *N.Y. Times*, Dec. 2, 4, and 5, 1942.

80. *Op. cit.*, in note 37, at 413.

81. 118 U.S. 375.

82. See my article, "The Power of Congress to Declare Peace," 18 *Mich. L.R.*, 669-75 (1920).

83. U.S. Code, tit. 22, §271. A vigorous attack was later made on the resolution's constitutionality by Representative Tinkham. *Cong. Record*, Feb. 5, 1935. Mr. David J. Lewis of Maryland introduced in the House on March 19, 1934, a similar measure to end, as he declared, "the impasse which has for years enabled thirty-three Senators to delay final action upon American membership in the World Court." *N.Y. Times*, Mar. 19, 1934.

84. *N.Y. Herald-Tribune*, Nov. 3, 1943.

85. *N.Y. Times*, Dec. 3, 1943.

86. *Ibid.*, Dec. 8, 1943.

87. *Ibid.*, Mar. 17, 1943.

88. *Ibid.*, Mar. 14, 1943.

89. *Ibid.*, Nov. 6, 1943.

90. *Ibid.*, June 22, 1920, quoted in Carl Brent Swisher, *American Constitutional Development*, 1.